David Stubbs enjoyed a varied career prior to establishing himself as a Management Training Consultant. His experiences include being a dental student, grave-digger, car salesman and RAF officer. He acted as Personnel Officer for Surrey County Council and then Management and Training Adviser at the Industrial Society. He was also Group Management Training Officer within the Ladbroke Group.

David Stubbs is a Member of the Institute of Training and Development and lives in Thornton Heath, Surrey.

David R. Stubbs

# ASSERTIVENESS AT WORK

**PAN BOOKS**

First published 1985 by Gower Publishing Co. Ltd
First published in paperback 1986 by Pan Books

This edition published 1997 by Pan Books
an imprint of Macmillan Publishers Ltd
25 Eccleston Place, London SW1W 9NF
and Basingstoke

Associated companies throughout the world

ISBN 0 330 35205 9

3 5 7 9 8 6 4 2

A CIP catalogue record for this book is available
from the British Library.

Typeset by CentraCet Limited, Cambridge
Printed and bound in Great Britain by
Mackays of Chatham plc, Chatham, Kent

# CONTENTS

## PART TWO
## COMMUNICATION SKILLS AND ASSERTION

# FOREWORD

by Professor John Adair

'Britain and America', runs the well-known tag, 'two nations divided by a common language'. Rarely do I feel that myself, but it is undeniable that we do occasionally use words in different ways. Take 'aggressive' as an example. For the British it carries overtones of unprovoked attack. American managers use it, however, as a compliment. To them the aggressive manager is one who shows energy or initiative; he is enterprising and self-assertive.

The concept of assertiveness is much more acceptable to us in Europe. Literally it means to state something confidently, without need for proof or regard for evidence. I do not care for the last implication – what university professor would? – but that is not what David Stubbs is talking about in this book. He is trying to get us not to be dogmatic but to have our own rights and opinions respected. There are times and places when we should insist on recognition of our claims. All too often we do not. We tend to understate ourselves. Without trying to be larger than life, we should be firm in putting our views and ourselves across. David calls upon us to be much more positive about ourselves in these ways. What is more to the point, he shows us how, and his book contains a wealth of examples to illustrate this sound advice. Like all good management books you will find it as relevant to family and social life as to the office or factory.

From my particular perspective of leadership studies I have a special reason for welcoming the book. Self-confidence strikes me as fundamental to leadership. Winston Churchill once defined courage as the virtue which makes possible all the other virtues. Well, I feel that way about self-confidence in leadership. Unless you have a degree of self-confidence it is difficult to see how you can conduct yourself, let alone other people.

Of course, self-confidence can degenerate into arrogance just as assertiveness can turn into aggressiveness. But David writes with such common sense and with such a firm purchase on human values that I do not think anyone can misunderstand his message on that score.

Not long ago I led a seminar on leadership for heads of university departments. 'What more would you like?' asked one of the questions on the evaluation sheet. Four out of the fifteen participants put down 'assertiveness training'. To me that underlines the real need for training in this area in every walk of managerial life. Many managers, especially those on the lower rungs of their career ladder, and those in middle management (who may feel they have been sliding down a 'snake' rather than going up a 'ladder'!), can benefit from assertiveness courses. I hope that this book will stimulate managers to seek out and make use of the courses available in this subject.

Lastly, on a personal note, may I welcome a new author into the field of management education and training. I have known David for some time and admired his contribution to leadership development. Writing one's first book is no easy task. Writing a first book as clear, readable and lively as *Assertiveness at Work* counts as a double achievement. I am sure it will add a new dimension to his own work as well as being a lasting contribution to the field. May I congratulate him on this book and welcome you, the reader, to the feast of stimulating ideas and practical advice that follows.

# PREFACE TO THE FIRST EDITION

From our early childhood we spend a lot of time consciously or subconsciously acquiring skills that will help us in life. We learn the effects of certain actions that we take.

- We learn all about the impression we give when we smile at people. Many of us have learned to smile at people we do not like so that we give one impression and hide another.
- We learn how we can affect people by wearing different clothes and how vital this can be to first impressions in both business and social life.
- We learn how to use the intonation of our voice subtly to modify the meaning of our words. We can sound aggressive and menacing, or gentle and soothing. We can even change the meaning of words completely. By saying 'Oh, that's just fine' in a sarcastic voice we can give the impression that things are terrible.

Although most of us have a high level of these skills, we often feel that we do not create the impression that we want. We would like to do better for ourselves and be perceived in a different light by others.

- We can feel that we have been manipulated; that someone got the better of us; that we lost.
- We can feel that, although we got what we wanted, our relationship with those concerned has suffered; that we cannot trust people when we are away; that we have not got their full co-operation; that they are waiting for their chance to 'get back at us'.
- We may have given the wrong impression, a poor impression, or not even made any impression.

Success in business and social life depends very much on the impression we make on others. These impressions are the basis for our relationships. Some people seem to have a natural gift for creating the right impression and relating well to others; it is a factor which organisations take into account when they select and develop employees who work in sales or jobs where they deal with others. It is also vital to management success, affecting relationships with subordinates and the manager's ability to represent the team.

A recent survey into 'trouble routes' for buses in London found that trouble arose as much from the personality and skills (or lack of them) of the bus conductor as from the routes. Some conductors always seemed able to cope with the situations they met whereas trouble followed others around. Similarly, successful managers seem to have an ability to form good impressions and relationships at work; they are the people who can meet the needs of situations as they arise.

# ABOUT THIS BOOK

The objective of this book is to give readers guidelines within which they can develop their own assertion and influence to suit their personality and circumstances. It differs from books and courses which are based on North American research and experience. It is the result of experience and training in the United Kingdom which proved that North American practice produced different impressions for the British. It takes account of the values, customs and habits peculiar to the British.

This book deals not only with what we can do, but how we can do it. We often have good intentions but cannot put them into practice for lack of guidelines and skill. Most of us can recall situations at work or in our social life where, for all our good intentions, our actions did not achieve the results we wanted.

It is intended for those who would like to be more effective in standing up for their rights, influencing others and handling difficult people and situations. Although it is written primarily for management, it applies to anyone who would like to improve these skills in life.

By increasing our awareness of:

- our own behaviour
- responses that we get
- choices of behaviour that we can use and
- responses to that behaviour

we can gradually modify our behaviour to suit occasions, improve relationships and gain more success in life.

The thinking and practice reflected in this book are based

on experience of running training courses and follow-up sessions in many organisations in Great Britain.

Many readers and, I hope, most managers will find that what is recommended in the book is their normal behaviour. For this I make no apology; that is how it should be with learning based on successful practice and experience.

For those who wish to check, or improve on, their skills, I would advise them to read a chapter at a time and relate it to their own experience. I have included a last chapter of hints for those who wish to add to the choices of behaviour that they can use with others.

David R. Stubbs
Leadership Publications and Training

# PREFACE TO THE SECOND EDITION

Since I wrote this book over ten years ago to suit our society — our society itself has changed:

- Many people, especially in cities and big towns, will have noticed that their local community spirit has deteriorated. I now have fewer neighbours whom I know and who reply to my routine (ritual, see Chapter 14) greetings. A 1996 report by Wimpey Homes analysing the psychology of home buyers for the mid 1990s states: 'Once inside, house buyers adopt a fortress mentality, opening the door only occasionally to let friends in or, one assumes, their partners out.' It cannot always be assumed that local people will be well disposed towards you and will welcome a friendly relationship.
- More people are ready to criticise bad service and goods and complain aggressively.
- Children and young people are more likely to rebel and show aggression and rejection against parental control, guidelines and standards.
- Most of us have experienced the development of a more self-centred culture, where people adopt a more aggressive stance in order to get on and get the results demanded of them.

- In 1996 the term road rage has been included in the dictionary covering aggressive behaviour by drivers towards others; ranging from gestures and verbal abuse to physical attacks. The 1996 *Lex Report on Motoring* states that almost three-quarters of drivers have been the victims of road rage.
- The employment practices of many of our work organisations have changed radically. There has been extensive redundancy taking place to cope with less demand, mergers or new technology or achieve increased profits and economies. Job security is becoming a memory for many. Some employees are now on short-term contracts working in organisations that depend for their survival on their own short-term contracts. Charles Handy, management guru and philosopher, examines these trends in his books. In the management ethos of 1996, with leaner teams, increased targets and more stress, aggression at work is more prevalent.

One effect is that many employees can now face a 'take it or leave it' situation with their management. Non-assertive employees will know exactly what I mean: as people working for the organisation diminish the work doesn't. They get additional duties and responsibilities. There are all the reasons for accepting them and saying yes as listed on page 132 plus the fact that they may have mortgages and children at local schools; they want to keep their jobs.

The problem arises if they get overworked, particularly if their programming is to 'do a good job'. This leads to stress and often a deterioration in their private lives. Also they resent it, but their poorer performance and sometimes increased sickness combined with longer working hours, with a less satisfactory personal life, can lead them to blame themselves. They can feel inadequate and that they can't cope with life. This means that they lose self-respect – one of the goals of assertiveness.

This is common when people deal with other people's stresses, emotions and demands. The American practice, if rich enough, is to hire a professional to listen to your problems and stresses. British people tend to take their problems and stresses home. What so often happens is that your partner, or friend, will do two things. They will either 'hijack' your problems by taking them over with their problems:

- I know just what you mean, I had a similar/worse experience . . .
- I know, what happened to me was . . .

and you end up listening to their problems, instead of reducing your stress. Or, even worse, the other person will suggest or even tell you what you should do about your particular difficulties which are causing you stress. Although well intentioned this leads to responses such as:

- It is rather different where I work
- You don't know what is involved
- It is not like that

and so on. Sometimes this can lead to an argument, thereby increasing the stress, rather than reducing it. The self-blame that can result can mean a loss of self-worth. After all, being able to live satisfactorily with others means being able to live with ourselves. It is ourselves with whom we live all of our lives, communicating mentally. Self-esteem and self-respect are the basis of a satisfying life.

The aggressive employee can become a team wrecker, who has a negative effect on customer relations and quality.

As a result of these trends, if you identify with one or more of them, the skills of assertiveness have become even more important:

- Making your point without making an enemy.
- Coping with criticism and manipulation.
- Reducing anger and emotion in others.
- Avoiding misunderstandings.
- Dealing with problems with empathy.
- Keeping problems with the owner.
- Getting quickly to the real facts.
- Saying no reasonably.
- Letting people know that they are giving you problems without giving offence.
- Giving yourself the best chance of changing the behaviour of others.

A cautionary note here: Assertiveness is only effective if both parties have a mutual respect. In other words, if the other person dislikes you and is aggressive then the assertive thing to do is to revert to other behaviour:

- If a gang of thugs with iron bars were approaching me, I would not stop to give an explanation of how I could not afford to be injured because I had not kept up with my medical insurance. I would use avoidance behaviour, assertively and I hope quickly.
- If somebody is not listening to me or not trying to understand my point of view, then I might use aggressive behaviour, quite rightly and assertively in order that my points of view are heard and considered.

Assertiveness is a concept which varies according to cultures and relationships. Its aim is to achieve self-respect and respect for others in our relationships and communication. To help with the theory and practice of this, I have added two more chapters. The first is to explain some concepts using the ideas of Tony Buzan in order to make them understandable and memorable. The second is to give some pointers on dealing with difficult people.

David Stubbs
Leadership Publications and Training
25, Springfield Road
Thornton Heath
Surrey CR7 8DZ
Tel: 0181–240–7118

# ACKNOWLEDGEMENTS

When I started to write this book I had a great desire to write down all I had learned and knew about the subject. How do we piece together our knowledge which we take for granted as being acquired personally; from books, conversation with others, observation of life?

Inevitably I have plagiarised widely, often not from an original source but from secondary sources or others that are even further removed. As I often find in running training courses, many ideas which I have spent hours conceiving are written and practised elsewhere in the world and were always there for me to pick up.

I would like to thank the following influences and sources who have all contributed immensely to this book:

Dr Julian Feinstein – my colleague of Leadership Publications and Training, also L.D.L.

Leonard Seymour Smith – of Eurocomm Associates

Tony Everist – Ladbroke Group Training

Professor John Adair – Professor of Leadership Studies, Surrey University, Guildford

and especially my colleague – Sandra (Sandy) Ellvers Dix of Leadership Publications and Training.

Also, all the many people on my training courses and all those from whose knowledge and work I have gained directly or indirectly.

DRS

PART ONE

# BEHAVIOUR AND RELATIONSHIPS

# 1

# BEHAVIOUR AND EFFECTS

We have all been 'programmed' or 'conditioned' to some extent by our early upbringing, our experiences and society. We know what we consider to be right, correct or good behaviour in certain circumstances.

## LEARNING BEHAVIOUR

When we are very young we are constantly being subjected to admonitions to do this and not to do that. We are told when our behaviour is 'good' and are rewarded with supportive words and actions. We can easily recognise the shaping behaviour of parents with their babies; so-called 'good' behaviour, which may be just a matter of the babies keeping quiet, or not expressing themselves, can be rewarded with smiles, soft encouraging voices and perhaps presents. It is generally accepted that we develop many of our personality and behaviour traits during our very early upbringing.

Later on, when children start to think for themselves, other influences come into play. The children may find that their experiences may be in conflict with their early 'programming'. The very spoilt child may find that behaviour which was 'all right' at home is not supported, or is actually condemned, by peers and teachers at school. They can equally find their behaviour supported, for example, when the aggressive child finds that bullying others at school gains rewards and is not censured by the teachers. Children will continue such behaviour if they meet with success and approval, leaving the other children to face the problem of coping with them.

Children who find that later experiences and influences do not conform with what they have learnt as accepted behaviour may try to adapt in order to meet with success and approval. Experience has shown that without support and help this can be a long painful process. There can be many other reactions such as:

- exaggerating the behaviour which does not meet with approval
- attempts to avoid situations where conflict and disapproval arise
- not expressing themselves honestly in these situations or being ready to change if they meet with opposition

all of which can meet with some success and perhaps limited approval.

- By exaggerating the difference the children can feel they are standing up for themselves, and may even get their own way.
- By avoiding situations, or not expressing themselves, they can be successful in avoiding conflict.
- By not expressing themselves honestly, or changing their views to suit those of others, they may get approval. This may only be short term because they may sacrifice long-

term respect. In this case an attitude of 'What can I do about it?' or martyrdom can still give a feeling of limited success because conflict has been avoided.

This process is continued through life, other significant phases being further education away from home and experiences at work. In these situations we are faced with new influences which can change our behaviour and, therefore, our perceived personality.

## PERSONALITY AND BEHAVIOUR

Most of us find it very hard to change our personality and behaviour when we get older; instead we fall back on old techniques. If we cannot adopt behaviour that allows for success without incurring disapproval and possible conflict with others we may:

- exaggerate our differences with others
- minimise our differences with others or make them less perceptible
- avoid our differences with others

Every individual is different, as are their upbringings and experiences. Even in the same family such factors as parental favouritism can have a significant effect on children. So we evolve our own personality which results in individual perceptions of similar situations. Managers may well have experienced many different kinds of behaviour in response to their attempts to treat everyone equally: the manager who comes across an employee glancing at a newspaper during working hours and says in a reasonable even tone:

- 'Please get on with your work'

may well get reactions as diverse as:

- 'Are you implying I don't work hard enough?' (said aggressively).
- 'Come on, at the rate we work we deserve five minutes for the paper' (challengingly).
- 'Okay boss' (said evenly or cheerfully with a return to work).
- 'I work as hard as anyone round here' (said in a resentful or hurt voice).
- Silence (with compliance and possibly a hint of resentment).
- 'Oh sorry – I won't do it again' (in a pleading voice).
- 'Just wanted to check the football results to see if I could afford to leave this place' (cheekily).
- Tears.
- 'Now then – your work will get done' (said patronisingly).

The list is endless.

We tend to develop our own 'set' of reactions to given situations in life, these reactions being perceived by others as our personality. Similarly, we can imagine the probable reaction of others, whom we know, when we behave in a certain way, based on our perceptions of their personality. We can also think of how we behave with these different people when they treat us in known ways, our reaction being modified according to the relationship that we have with the other person.

# TERRITORIAL SPACE

We all have 'territory' or 'personal space' which we vary for different types of relationships.

- Suppose that you arrived at a beach on which there was one other person who was sitting in the middle . . . where would you choose to sit?
- Or if you were that single person on the beach and another person came and sat right beside you . . . what would be your reaction?
- Most of us, considering the other person to be a stranger, would try to create and maintain a 'distance' which would allow us to be comfortable. We would like to be at that distance where we would feel that a stranger was not intruding on our privacy.
- What would be your reaction if the other person was someone whom you liked very much and knew well . . . would this 'distance' change?
- What would be your reaction if the other person was someone whom you did not know well but would like to know better . . . does this change your tactics and choice of 'distance'?

Our relationship or lack of it would determine whether we sat next to them, near them, away from them, or left the scene. Our wishes to change our relationship can also affect this distance.

Some psychologists have categorised the distance or 'space' within which we are comfortable with others into main zones:

- Public – for strangers
- Social – for many people we work or deal with; shop-keepers; acquaintances
- Personal – for friends
- Intimate – for very close friends and relationships

Research has shown that comfortable distances within these categories vary for different ethnic groups, nationalities and, broadly, for countries. The British tend to be more distant and have less physical contact than, for instance, Latin races; Latins have more contact in greeting each other and can disconcert or even offend the British by their seeming lack of distance.

As our relationships get closer, so we allow others closer to us and there is more bodily contact. Someone who wants to improve a relationship with you will try to get closer to you; think about your behaviour with your good friends, starting with your first meeting. People who are happy to have a lot of casual physical contact when they are talking together, even with others, give the idea that their relationship is close.

# INVASION OF SPACE AND EFFECTS

Problems arise if somebody invades our space by getting closer than our territorial or permitted distance.

- When strangers get too close to us in lifts, crowded trains or buses, we have to pretend that they are 'non-people'. If we make direct eye contact, the normal way of recognising a person, we have to look away. We cannot acknowledge strangers within our permitted distance or 'space' as people and we shut our reactions down. We become like mindless robots on the outside, whatever thoughts we have on the inside, that is, unless we do know them, in which case we have to try and move to our distance to be comfortable.

One of the ways in which people can threaten others or make them uncomfortable is by invading their permitted space. It is exactly the same with animals and territory. We know the reactions of most household pets when another animal moves uninvited into its territory. A similar situation can arise when people lose their tempers with others. They can move closer aggressively, wag a finger close to the other person, or even forcibly make bodily contact. The reaction of the other person to this physical invasion of their space in an aggressive manner is usually 'fight', 'flight' or resentful submission. We only have to think of parents getting angry with their children and the reactions of different children.

The invasion of physical space may not be intentionally aggressive. Studies have been carried out in libraries and hospitals about people sitting too close to others. The reactions were mainly resentment, shown by uncomfortable behaviour, flight, shown by people getting up and moving away and, less often, fight, shown by hostile remarks. Again, if we think of our reaction in train compartments when it seems that our space has been invaded, we can appreciate that people getting inside our permitted or wanted distance cause similar feelings inside us.

## PSYCHOLOGICAL SPACE

In exactly the same way as we, like animals, have territorial space, so we, as thinking beings, have mental or psychological space, involving our minds, values, beliefs, thoughts and feelings. It is usually accompanied or reinforced by physical space behaviour, for example in the way we lean closely towards someone to whisper an intimacy that is permitted by our relationship. The total reaction we have to someone is a combination of how we react to their physical behaviour and mental approach.

The type of relationship we have with others affects what we allow people to say to us without our being offended. It determines the amount of familiarity we allow people. Think of the last time you were slightly upset by someone – was it because they 'overstepped the mark' in your eyes? Spoken communication is usually reinforced by non-verbal communication, bringing into play physical space limits. We thus have mental as well as physical boundaries determining our psychological zones and boundaries with others. We can call this our 'personal space'.

## PERSONAL SPACE

This personal space can vary for different people and in different relationships. Think about the freedom of expression and the familiarity you would allow:

- a complete stranger
- a shopkeeper you use regularly on a business-like footing

- a work colleague with whom you only have business dealings
- a social acquaintance
- a friend
- a close friend
- an intimate friend

Members of families have been known to adopt most of these relationships with each other, according to how they get on together. We allow friends more leniency; we allow them closer to us.

A close relationship has its own danger; the closer we allow people, the more they can hurt us – we are more vulnerable. In exactly the same way as you can ignore someone who is aggressive if you have physical space or distance between yourselves, so you can ignore people who do not have a close permanent relationship with you. The stranger who says something offensive and aggressive such as 'Well if you do that you'd be an idiot – you have no chance of success' can be ignored more easily than a trusted friend and adviser.


# INVASION OF PERSONAL SPACE AND EFFECTS

Overstepping the permitted personal boundaries in relationships is achieved by a combination of physical and psychological 'space' invasion. It normally leads to the same reactions of fight, flight or resentful submission. It leads to a breakdown in communications. We can feel angry, hurt, wounded, offended, or resentful if somebody 'oversteps the mark' with us.

- A recent guidebook for Italians intending to emigrate to Australia gave the advice not to call Australians 'bastards'. Although this word is colloquially used as a friendly term among Australian men, it would be unlikely to be accepted as such from an Italian immigrant. The behaviour would be over the limit.

- The British House of Commons has well-defined rules on terms by which members can address each other. Although to many of us it often sounds on the radio like a juvenile 'free for all', many members who have been apparently slanging each other in public in an offensive way have good working relationships in joint committees. Their behaviour is within the permitted limits.

- We have a range of names which denote personal distance and formality:
  − our title Mr, Mrs, Miss, Ms, with our surname
  − our surname on its own
  − our first name
  − diminutives of first names and nicknames
  − pet or intimate names

  If we read the personal columns of the British press on St Valentine's Day we can appreciate the broad range of intimate names that may well be known only to the two people involved in the relationship. If you have one of these names it is not normally acceptable if it is used by a chance acquaintance. Have you got a personal name that would embarrass you if others knew it?

- The names we allow others to use is a sign of the distance we want to maintain. In the military services the very formal 'Sir' or 'Ma'am' is used. Schools use a range of formal titles. (Nicknames of a derogatory or friendly kind are found in these establishments for those in authority but are usually not used in face-to-face communication with the person involved.)

- We know the different names that we can be called in our relationships to indicate approval and disapproval. Love and friendliness is indicated by the use of our less formal names accompanied by a suitable tone of voice and closer physical behaviour. Disapproval is indicated by the use of a more formal name, accompanied by a complementary tone of voice and more formal and distant behaviour.

We have well-defined personal boundaries in our relationships and are skilled in using our communication to get attention or convey our moods by different tactics using these personal space factors.

# RIGHTS

Our life space concerns our personal rights which we have as people. Within society all people are not equal, but we have the right to be treated equally up to a basic level of respect for fellow humans. There are many laws, systems and religions which embody this principle. In Britain it is enshrined in the Magna Carta, the Mother of Parliaments, Speakers' Corner and so on; there have been recent laws about racialism and equal opportunities; many wars have been fought to keep our freedom, and yet the British today are not always good at standing up for their rights as individuals.

Flight, fight or resentful submission characterise the reactions of the British to many situations found in management or life.

- If the food or service in a restaurant is poor, the typical British reaction is generally to avoid a 'scene'. Most people will not complain to the management for fear of either appearing aggressive or getting an aggressive response. They normally complain to others at the table and may even drop hints to the person giving the service, which can be ignored. If the offence is bad enough they will avoid returning to the restaurant.

In this example the people in the restaurant have not stood up for their rights. They are happy to pay for a good service or meal, but when they do not receive it they do not express themselves honestly because they cannot think of a way without seeming offensive or risking a rebuff.

We can compare this with the habit of diners in North America or the Continent where different customs and habits prevail. Poor service or food is more likely to provoke an instant complaint or request.

The British manager is often faced with the same problem at work. Subordinates do not measure up to the manager's standards in one or more aspects of their job. The manager may:

1. Say nothing to the subordinate but tell his or her colleagues about the deficiencies, basing their actions on the principle that they fear the subordinate's reaction. It may put a strain on the relationship between the manager and subordinate as they have to work together on other matters each day. The frustration in these managers can build up until eventually they do explode and then revert to option 3, to the shock of the subordinate.

2. Have a talk with subordinate, where the deficiencies may be hinted at with varying degrees of strength. There is

always the danger that the message may not be clear enough to be understood or, may, if the subordinate wants, be ignored. Usually it is 'wrapped up' with a lot of other matters which are not particularly relevant, as a sort of 'sugaring of the pill'. This wrapping can be used to distract attention by both parties from the real message, which is thus diluted.

Even if the hint is clear, if it elicits an aggressive response (sometimes involving the trade union) the manager will back down.

However, the subordinate is usually not clear what the point of the talk was, although the manager is sure that he/she has clarified the situation.

3. Have a talk with the subordinate in which matters are not minced. Plain speaking is the order of the day. The manager tells the subordinate of the deficiencies and what they should do to correct them.

This will work if the subordinate is submissive enough, but may arouse resentment and can lead to instant confrontation. It is the traditional method for many parents with young children who are below the age of reason. It is well known that it becomes less effective as the children grow up and start thinking for themselves. Even when it works, the child's resentment is easily detected.

# CLASSES OF BEHAVIOUR

These three common forms of behaviour can be categorised as follows:

- *Avoidance behaviour* tries to ignore any violation of your own rights, usually for fear of the reaction of others. It consists of evading any honest confrontation, often by flight.

- *Accommodating behaviour* expresses your views, thoughts and feelings in such a way either that they can be disregarded, misconstrued or that others may take advantage of you. It usually has the avoidance of conflict as its goal.

Avoidance and accommodation could both be classed as 'non-assertion'.

- *Aggressive behaviour* offends or violates another person's rights. It involves overstepping the mark. It can occur as a result of a build up of offence, as a result of 'the last straw that broke the camel's back', or because of doubts about self-worth or ability to control a situation. It expresses itself in a way that will invade another's personal (physical/psychological) space.

We can see that these categories of behaviour are decided by our determination or reluctance to protect our own personal space and by the reactions of others. None of these behaviours is wrong as such. We can think of situations where they are appropriate.

- There is a well known saying that it is often 'better to run away, to live and fight another day'. Some problems do resolve themselves if left alone.
- Often a gentle hint is a good way of bringing up a point about someone's behaviour, which they then change.
- I was once at Rome airport with my wife, who had a broken leg in plaster. On arrival there was no sign of the wheelchair I had arranged for. I queued at the desk and politely asked the harassed clerk for the wheelchair. I was

assured it would be there. Finally, I made a scene, ranting and raving at the clerk. This got instant reaction; three wheelchairs appeared and we made the London plane with seconds to spare. We were first off the plane at London and were met with a wheelchair. It seemed that my aggressive behaviour suited the situation.

# 2

# BEHAVIOUR AT WORK

In the last chapter we saw how behaviour can be categorised as avoidance, accommodating (non-assertion) or aggressive. We can recognise these behaviours at work. Many managers use them in order to change people's behaviour or thoughts at work. Organisations may even have a 'management style' which is based on the predominance of these types of behaviour.

## NON-ASSERTIVE STYLE

In organisations with a non-assertive management style there will be comments such as:

- 'Nobody can get sacked here – you would have to do something amazing like . . .'
- 'I can't do anything, my manager won't back me up.'
- 'I hardly ever see my manager and I never see the Director.'
- 'I don't know why I'm on this management course – I just got a memo telling me to attend,' or
- 'My manager said it could be a good idea.'

- 'We don't need to appraise staff – I'm sure that they have some idea of how they are doing.'
- 'I think I would know if my boss thought that I was doing badly.'

As somebody who has run many management training courses I am surprised at how often delegates (apparently) have very different impressions of their work performance and success from those of their managers, who may have briefed me 'in confidence'.

A common reaction to 'difficult' people and problems in these organisations is to ignore them for as long as possible, in the hope that the problems will solve themselves. If this does not work then the next recourse is to change the organization to accommodate the problem. This can involve changing a person's job, so that the part where they are not successful is minimised, restructuring the section or department to minimise the problem or even moving the problem to another section or department without solving it. Of course if it is a difficult person the favoured solution is for them to join a different organisation, especially if this can be brought about without any trouble.

The non-assertive approach of some organisations can have many advantages such as:

- People can and often do solve their own problems without management intervention.
- There is a good level of security.
- People can use their strengths in their jobs.
- Using accommodating behaviour avoids arguments and bad feelings at work.
- It works with people who are accommodating at work – a

light hint may be enough to make a point where an aggressive approach may get bad results.

However, anybody who has worked in one of these organisations may find disadvantages such as:

- a lack of overall achievement and results
- a lack of teamwork, with everybody doing their own thing
- a high level of frustration
- poor management—employee communications, with a strong 'grapevine'
- a lack of success with aggressive employees (which could involve trade unions)

We may know many non-assertive managers who may be quite successful in the right organization with self-motivated, high quality employees. Some typical forms of their behaviour are:

- always apologising for any possible offence
- very wordy, especially if discussing anything that could be thought personal
- over-justifying any action or statement
- always considering another plan rather than being decisive
- hesitant, pleading, monotonous or quiet voice when speaking
- short eye contact, frequently looking away
- they avoid 'rocking the boat', will tend to be swayed by the current speaker into adapting their own ideas, and will do a lot for a 'quiet life'.

# AGGRESSIVE STYLE

In organisations with an aggressive management style there will be comments such as:

- 'We're only interested in results.'
- 'It's the bottom line that matters.'
- 'Don't give me those problems – we can get plenty of good staff to work for us.'
- 'We don't send people on courses – we're too busy doing the job.'
- 'I may be autocratic (straightforward/straightspeaking) but it works.'
- 'Nice people don't win.'
- 'You've got to lay it on the line for people.'

Managers in these organisations will act immediately at the first sign of a problem. These organisations often have an appraisal system or performance review which are used to highlight weaknesses and set targets. In these organisations people either shape up or get out. There may be training courses but they are likely to take the form of lectures on what employees should do or ought to do and may well turn into a sort of short intense organisation 'brainwashing'.

An aggressive approach has some advantages in that:

- it often gets results for management
- it is successful with non-assertive people
- management tell employees what they want
- it can give short-term satisfaction

On the other hand it may have disadvantages such as:

- employees may resent aggressive behaviour in the long term
- there will probably be many disputes, bad feelings and power struggles
- communication is one-way – ideas and suggestions are rarely offered to management
- it can engender counter-aggression (possibly involving trade unions)

Again we may know many aggressive managers who may achieve success in the right sort of organisation. Indeed, some organisations look for an aggressive approach in their business and therefore in their management. It can be successful with staff who are very obedient 'company' or organisation people. With self-motivated questioning employees, however, there will tend to be clashes, and unless the employees become managers in the organisation they may well leave to try to achieve it in another (possibly competitive) organisation. Some typical examples of the behaviour of aggressive managers are that they are:

- heedless of other people's feelings at work ('I'm not in the popularity business!')
- prepared to state their needs and opinions forcefully
- prone to use threats directly or implicitly ('We're in the business of . . .' or 'We're not in the business to . . .' etc.)
- quick to blame others and sarcastic
- emphatic in their manner of speaking
- users of direct eye contact to the point of staring

# BEHAVIOUR CHANGE

You may be able to identify the sort of manager who is prevalent in your organisation or department, although many people say that managers change their behaviour to suit the situations they meet.

- Some managers may be accommodating to some people at work, provided the managers get the respect and authority they feel they deserve. This non-assertive behaviour can change to aggression with those who do not respect their authority or ability.
- In some organisations aggressive senior management may demand accommodating (submissive, obedient) behaviour in their dealings with middle management, while expecting them to be aggressive to junior employees.
- Many managers, especially in hierarchical organisations, often treat those below them as not worth the normal respect they would give to a valued human. They can insult them directly or indirectly, for example by:
    - keeping juniors waiting until the manager is ready without explanation
    - allowing interruptions of whatever nature when the junior is talking with them, without checking the priority
    - interrupting a junior's concentration when working, often with simple matters that could wait

These are common sights that show management's subconscious attitude to employees' rights at work. Much worse can occur. How many of us can think back to incidents at work when we were insulted by a manager in a way that would be completely unacceptable in our social lives?

- Some managers who are predominantly aggressive or non-assertive at work can behave in the opposite way at home.

Most people I have met in management can be non-assertive or aggressive in order to deal with situations they encounter. Many of them say that they are tolerant up to a point. This could be interpreted as being non-assertive or accommodating up to a certain point, beyond which they will show aggression. There is a tradition in Britain of praising and encouraging non-assertive behaviour in family life, schools, religion and when you start work. Such qualities as loyalty, humility (or at least not being boastful), obedience, tolerance and conformity are regarded as good in early family programming and are later reinforced by social conditioning.

Many people from other countries comment on the amount of times the British say 'excuse me' or 'sorry', even to the point of apologising when we bump into a chair or table. Such behaviour is not bad in itself as long as it is appropriate; it is reasonable, if you are going to push by someone, that you say 'excuse me' before you intrude into their permitted physical space; it shows a respect for others as humans that can be missing in some societies.

However, it has also been noted that the British can be stubborn, aggressive enemies when aroused.

## THE MANAGEMENT DILEMMA

Many supervisors I know, when they have been placed in a management position for the first time, have been faced with a dilemma. Do they change their relationship with their former workmates? Do they distance themselves, behave aggressively or try to keep their previous behaviour as one of the team? It is the same argument as to whether managers should be task-oriented or people-oriented.

There are many books that suggest that the manager's job is to unite individuals successfully in a team which is capable of achieving the task. Professor John Adair's books and training even specify the actions that can be taken to accomplish these aims. This is very helpful to people in leadership positions, with the sole reservation that it is not always what you do (and say) but the way that you do (and say) it that matters.

A manager may decide that it would be a good idea to resolve some conflict within the team. This can be done either aggressively or non-assertively. This is true for many management (leadership) actions such as giving guidance, briefing, appraising, counselling and delegating with employees. Many such awkward situations at work entail conflict, expressed by argument, involving people's rights as humans. We can examine this in more detail.

# A BRITISH METHOD OF ARGUMENT

Professor Edward de Bono outlined a valuable concept in one of his television programmes about decision making. It concerns a British habit when presented with a different belief, idea, value, suggestion or practice (B) from your own (A). The other person usually stresses the advantages of their proposition and the weakness in your own (see Figure 2.1).

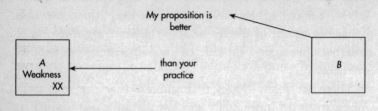

Figure 2.1

This criticism of the weaknesses in *A* may be only implicit, as shown in sentences containing words like 'you should' or 'you ought', followed by the proposition.

- e.g. *B*: 'You should reorganise your office with the files over there so that we don't have so far to walk every time we want one.'
- e.g. *B*: 'It would be better if you did that report today instead of spending (wasting?) time on a staff meeting.'

Your ideas, values, beliefs and practices are within your psychological space. It is these, if we are suffering from stresses and strains in life, that we have to rebuild, for which we need to be alone. After shocks, we often seek solitude to rethink our attitudes and values – we need to rebuild our personal space. The shock to the system can be good or bad, wanted or unwanted, such as falling in love or failing for the first time. Any unwelcome attack by another person on your views or practices is a form of aggression. In contrast, if you invite criticism, you have allowed the person closer to you psychologically and it is not, therefore, an invasion of space.

Some people can allow others, if they respect their

authority, to criticise them without feeling resentment, probably due to their early programming as children and their later social conditioning. Consider how *you* react when different people criticise you. Most of us do not like adverse criticism. We may well follow the advice if it is constructive and we can see the benefits, but we do not find the process of being criticised a pleasant experience.

The intensity of the attack is dependent on several factors.

- How close to you (permitted space) is the attacker? It is possible to ignore people at a distance. People near and dear to you can hurt you much more.
- Have you given permission (or do you allow) the criticism? or is it uninvited – an invasion of your personal space?
- How strongly you are attacked.

If the proposition *B* comes from someone you respect and is not too aggressive, or if you have invited it, the matter may be settled without dispute (see Figure 2.2).

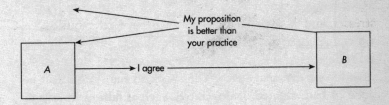

Figure 2.2

- e.g. 'Yes, it would save time to move the files there.'
- e.g. 'Yes, we didn't have much to discuss and the report is important.'

If the matter is not settled with genuine agreement it is because *B*'s proposal has been perceived as aggressive. Aggression, as discussed, is likely to get the response of:

- Resentful submission – which settles the matter as a win for *B*. 'Oh, I suppose so.' 'If you think it's best.'
- Flight – which leaves the matter unresolved or as a win for *B*. 'I'm too busy to look into it right now.' 'Leave it with me.'
- Fight – this can be defensive or aggressive.

If it is fight then you become less responsive to the views or practice *B* because your personal space has been invaded. You build a barrier round your thoughts. You are fighting for your rights and are likely to respond by stressing the advantages of *A* (defensive) and, if you can, the weaknesses of the proposition *B* (aggression) (see Figure 2.3).

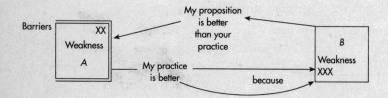

Figure 2.3

- e.g. *A*'s response: 'I prefer the files there because I don't use them much. I do use the VDU and that desk.'
- e.g. *A*'s response: 'That meeting is just as important as the report and I wouldn't be able to organise another one for two weeks.'

This defence of *A*, if combined with an attack on *B*, will in return provoke the traditional response to aggression. If the response is not avoidance or resentful submission (forms of capitulation), but to fight for the view or practice of proposition *B*, then we have got into an old-fashioned British argument. Both parties, *A* and *B*, are defending the advantages of their views or practice and attacking the other's weaknesses (see Figure 2.4).

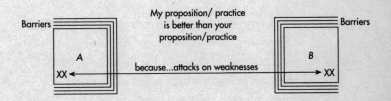

Figure 2.4

- e.g. *B*'s response: 'You still use the files quite a lot and I've never seen you use that bookcase.'
- e.g. *B*'s response: 'That report is very important when you compare it with what you get out of your staff meetings.'

Barriers are being erected between the two, to defend their own personal space against the attacks of the other. If one gives way it is seen as a loss for one and a win for the other. There is still the possibility of compromise, but it becomes more unlikely the longer the process goes on. The two participants tend more and more only to listen to each other for weaknesses in the other's argument. They pounce on any ammunition that they may use to try and win – which means there will be a loser, which is bound to cause resentment. I am sure that many of us will recognise that we have done this ourselves.

If there is not enough weakness in the other's case, then outside weaknesses such as personality or previous situations may be brought in (see Figure 2.5).

- e.g. *A*: 'I have read and use those books a lot, unlike you who has never had any training in decision making.'

  e.g. *B*: 'And I'm very glad I haven't if it means that I can't even see what is obvious to everybody.'

- e.g. *A*: 'Those reports just get glanced at filed but at least my team get to know what's going on from my meetings, which is more than you can say.'

  e.g. *B*: 'Look, we're paid to produce the reports not to conduct group therapy sessions.'

This can continue until communication breaks down totally.

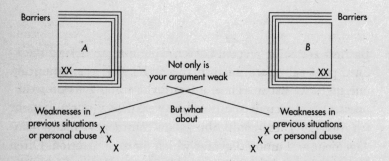

Figure 2.5

Many of us have experienced this when we have got into a position where we have stopped speaking with someone else. There is an angry silence, an atmosphere that 'you could cut with a knife', and we cannot back down.

These debates, arguments and/or negotiations can be resolved:

- If one wins by strength of argument or by use of power/authority. This will cause resentment in the loser who may well resurrect that argument at a later date.
- If a compromise is reached, sometimes involving a (neutral?) third party. This usually involves some formula based on

$$\frac{A + B}{2}$$

There may be different weightings for $A$ and $B$ which could alter the balance of the decision for or against one of the arguments. It results in neither party getting exactly what he/she wanted. They have both partly lost. This can cause bitterness if the compromise is reached after a communications breakdown.

There are resulting 'scars' which again may cause some arguments to be reopened later. The unresolved or unsatisfied parts of the argument may well be used as ammunition in the next battle. They are brought up as outside weaknesses if participants run out of weaknesses in the current argument. These compromises are common in many management and union disputes which go to arbitration. Often both sides claim a 'victory' when it would seem to the impartial that both have lost.

This method of argument, which most British can recognise both at home and work, involves problems of space and relationships. Even if we resolve the dispute in either of these ways it affects our subsequent relationships. It becomes a barrier to becoming more open with a person.

# ASSERTION

As humans we have an alternative to the traditional responses of

- fight (aggression)
- flight (avoidance)
- or resentful submission (accommodation)

This alternative is *assertive behaviour*, which involves protecting your life-space and rights while respecting those of others. It enables you and others to keep your self-esteem. In relies on being honest with people from the start – not as a last resort. Compare this with 'normal management practice'. It should lead to better relationships and understanding. The respect for others is not expressed as deference, appeasement, apology or self-effacement, which are non-assertive behaviours.

# Collaboration and synergy

In the same way as the British feel resentment which expresses itself as 'injured pride', the Japanese are very aware of 'loss of face'. Professor de Bono says that often a Japanese with an idea, suggestion, belief, idea or practice B will approach you by looking for good points in your *A*. This enables you to look for the good points in *B*'s case (see Figure 2.6).

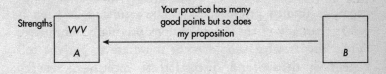

Figure 2.6

- e.g. *B*: 'I know you don't use the files so much now but I think it would save time if we moved the cabinet nearer.'
- e.g. *B*: 'I recognise that your staff meetings are valuable to you and your team but I feel that management views your report as a greater priority.'

Both sides are trying to win, but mutually.

Weakness in both arguments can now be jointly dealt with and may result in a better solution, *C* (see Figure 2.7).

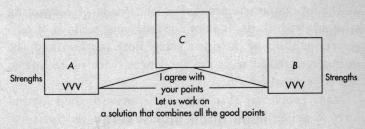

Figure 2.7

- e.g. *A*'s response: 'Yes, although I don't use the files so much, it would still save time if I changed the cabinet and the bookcase round.'

- e.g. *A*'s response: 'Well, I could keep the meeting down
    to half an hour and finish the report today.'

This process is called 'synergy', which is a word which
expresses unified group energy. The resulting decision is
better than any of the single options originally submitted.
Surely this is what should occur if we are to get the full
benefit of debate and discussion at meetings. Synergy
requires assertiveness and therefore a degree of skill from
participants.

## Workable compromise

Of course it is not always possible to attain the solution
that is the 'best of all worlds', just as it is not always
possible to get a unanimous decision at a meeting. The next
best solution is consensus or workable compromise. This is
not the same as majority, which leaves differences unresolved, but is based on acceptance if full agreement cannot
be reached.

The workable compromise is the result of bargaining
with assertive skills. It does not hurt your feelings of self-
respect or those of the other party. Both parties should be
mutually satisfied with the agreement, with no feeling of
loss of personal esteem.

Many people say that they are happy with their general
level of skills. Often this is because it is a very personal
matter and we tend to defend our actions, practices and
values – remember *A*!

Generally we can see our non-assertive or aggressive
behaviour as suiting most people and situations. They often
work in the short term, although many find that there are

long-term disadvantages. Assertiveness and influencing skills are needed for the difficult people and situations in life. They can be learnt if you perceive the need, want to change and are willing to try. It requires us to look honestly within ourselves.

# PATTERNS OF BEHAVIOUR

We all use different types of behaviour to suit different situations. The questions below are intended to help you understand which behaviour you *normally* use in given situations so that you can get an indication of the behaviour you prefer. It is not subject to marks or any such seemingly scientific approach, but should give you material so that you can look at your (instinctive) behaviour that affects your relationships with others.

If you have not met the specific situation given, then you cannot answer the question; however, try to think about your behaviour in a similar 'situation'. If you vary your behaviour in the given situation (i.e. no normal behaviour) then you can think about whether your behaviour leads to more understanding, a mutually agreeable solution and a better relationship.

## Non-assertive behaviour: avoidance or accommodating

- Do you have difficulty expressing your (real) feelings to others?
- Do you feel that you are often manipulated by others?

- Do you usually keep quiet when someone 'queue jumps' in front of you?
- Do you keep quiet or only complain to your friends and colleagues
    - if you get bad service or food in a restaurant?
    - if someone is disturbing you by talking loudly in a cinema or theatre?
- Do you often find yourself 'landed' or 'lumbered' with 'voluntary' tasks that you do not really want to do (i.e. they are not specifically anybody's duty)?
- Do you find it difficult to stand up to seniors, supervisors, authorities when you disagree with them?
- Do you avoid confronting people because you have to work with them tomorrow or you don't want to upset or anger them?
- Do you prefer to give subtle hints to people about your wishes? If so, which people and why?
- Are there situations in life which recur where you really would like to speak your mind?
- Do you often seem to change your mind to go along with the majority of a powerful group when really you don't altogether agree with them?
- Do you believe in 'Anything for a quiet life'?
- Do you find it difficult to cope with aggressive verbal behaviour?
- If attacked (verbally) do you resort to making excuses? In what tone of voice?
- Are there many situations which you 'suffer in silence', to which you have resigned yourself?

N.B. Many people who are normally non-assertive have a point beyond which they adopt aggressive behaviour.

# Aggressive behaviour

- Do you like to speak your mind openly, even if it may give offence to others?
- Would you describe yourself as blunt and to the point?
- Do you often get into arguments with others which are not resolved?
- Do you believe that 'attack is the best form of defence'?
- Do you easily lose your temper?
- Are you always ready to complain:
    - if you get bad service or food in a restaurant?
    - if you get faulty goods from a shop? In what tone of voice?
- Do you get angry and tell him/her off when someone queue jumps in front of you?
- Do you tell people who annoy you to shut up?
- Do you find yourself staring people down – sometimes/often?
- Do you tend to keep others waiting for you without any apology or reason?
- Do you take phone calls without reference to subordinates who are seeing you in your office?
- Do you criticise and find fault with others openly?
- Do you regularly try to get 'one up' on people?
- Do you feel that if you are reasonable with people you will probably end up giving something away?
- If attacked (verbally) do you resort to attacking the other person? In what tone of voice?
- Do you regard yourself as someone who does not 'suffer fools gladly'?
- Do you normally try very hard to get your solutions to other people's problems accepted?

# Assertive behaviour

- Can you express your feelings openly and honestly to people?
    - When was the last occasion that you did this?
    - Did it lead to more understanding and a better relationship?
- Do you mix (and get accepted) equally easily with superiors, peers and subordinates – at work and socially?
- Do you try and see the other person's point of view in arguments and discussions – do you acknowledge their point of view?
- Do you keep your temper when other people attack you?
- Do you find you can resolve most problems that other people cause you without damaging your relationship? Is the relationship better?
- Do you normally deal with your concerns and those of others rather than ignoring them or diverting them?
- Do you try to help others to work out their problems rather than imposing your solution?
- Do you try to resolve differences with people by bringing them out into the open.
- Do you normally
    - get bad food or service in a restaurant corrected without fuss?
    - get faulty goods replaced without fuss?
- Do you ask for money owing from people calmly?
- Do you correct people who queue jump in front of you in an even voice?
- Do you find you can count on people you know to collaborate with you?

# SUMMARY

We have looked at personal rights (space), as well as at types of behaviour which:

- ignore the personal rights of others (aggression)
- may lead to ours being ignored (non-assertion)
- respect our own and others' rights (assertion)

We have also said that any of these behaviours may be judged to be right, depending on the situation. Most managers can cope with everyday problems to their own satisfaction. It is when they have to deal with difficult people and situations that they may be limited if they can only respond with non-assertive or aggressive responses.

Areas at work where we may have problems such as:

- difficult subordinates, colleagues or bosses
- getting co-operation from others
- stating your real feelings and case
- always getting put upon and lumbered with work
- finding yourself blamed unfairly
- always losing discussions and arguments
- always having to check on people to whom you have given instructions

may be situations where assertiveness is likely to get better results than other forms of behaviour. It is not a matter of being assertive all the time, but of increasing your range of behaviour. Assertiveness gives the manager an additional option.

Many managers I have worked with confuse assertiveness

with aggression, and some confuse it with non-assertiveness. When you examine precisely what they say and do it is apparent that they may have the right intention but lack the skill to carry it out. Time and again I have heard managers say such things as:

- 'I have tried every approach possible'
- 'It's no good – you can do nothing with that person'
- 'You can't change them – believe me, I've tried'
- 'I was assertive – I told him exactly what was wrong with him – I believe in being honest'
- 'I was assertive – they couldn't fail to get the message'
- 'When he/she is in that sort of mood there is no way you can change his/her mind'

but found that they had not been assertive. After training, some of these managers were able to resolve their problems completely. Many were able to solve them partly, while most of those who had no success had not tried an assertive approach.

PART TWO

# COMMUNICATION SKILLS AND ASSERTION

# 3

# GOOD COMMUNICATION

The crucial factor in how we get on with people is how well we communicate with each other. This decides our relationship and therefore the permitted space we allow others and that they allow us. Consider the following.

You are flying near a foreign country where it is alleged that the government and a terrorist movement are committing atrocities against each other. Suddenly the pilot's voice comes over the intercom to say that the plane is being forced by fighters to land at an airport in that country.

After landing you are rounded up into trucks by heavily armed soldiers shouting at you in a language you don't understand. You are taken to a hotel and put into separate rooms.

Eventually your door crashes open and a huge, scowling solider, festooned with grenades and carrying a sub-machine-gun, bursts in and shouts in the foreign language at you.

- How would you feel? Most of us would be apprehensive, to say the least! Anyway, as you don't know how to respond in the foreign language you try to say that you are British, and hit upon the idea of showing him your passport. He takes the passport, looks at it, and then in impeccable English says, 'Ah, so you really are British, I lived in Britain for ten years.'

- Does this change your feelings? He then looks at your occupation in the passport and asks where you work. When you tell him he smiles and says 'Really, I worked there for two years.'
- How would you feel now – would it be different from your first feeling?

The story could be extended to include mutual friends, acquaintances and experiences. The point is to demonstrate that our non-verbal and verbal communication determine our relationships. Let's consider some aspects of the story.

## UNDERSTANDING AND WAVELENGTH

The first element was whether you could establish a common language, which was helped or hindered by the non-verbal communication of appearance, dress, expression and so on. You can similarly find yourself 'put off' because you are on a different wavelength; for example, they could be speaking in English but using grammar and vocabulary that is different from your own. Factors such as status symbols, accent, dress and expression can reinforce these differences in wavelength. If you have ever been in the company of people who are talking about a shared expertise which you don't have, you will know what I mean. Similarly in social life you know how uncomfortable it is if you feel 'like a fish out of water' or if everybody talks 'above your head'.

The relationships between some managers and their workforces often demonstrate this. The manager may be more interested in the future, plans, objectives and talking, the workforce more interested in activity, rewards and doing. These differences are often emphasised by different places of work, clothes and places to eat.

It is worth considering the practice of some Japanese industries where there is much more communication and agreement than in Britain. The managers can be found wearing the same clothes as the workforce, eating in the same canteens and spending a lot of time on the shop-floor.

Words are just symbols which we use in combinations, together with non-verbal communication, to express our thoughts, ideas, beliefs and values. The communication is understood when the listener (or reader) can distil our exact meaning from our words. This is much easier where those involved are on the same wavelength insomuch as they use the same meanings for the same words and the non-verbal communication is appropriate. Local government, the civil service and legal services probably sacrifice most citizens' empathy* because of their tendency to use a different language, be it 'officialese' or legal jargon.

## ESTABLISHING COMMON GROUND

The second element in communication is establishing common ground. In the story it was achieved by sharing common experience but it can be achieved in a number of different ways.

It is not enough for two or more people to have a

---

* Empathy: ability to comprehend another person fully. Whereas sympathy is to *have the same* feeling or opinion as another, empathy is the power to *understand* another person's feeling or opinion.

common language when communicating well with each other; there is also a need for co-operation. This implies looking for some agreement rather than emphasising differences between minds (as discussed earlier in 'A British method of argument', page 25.)

A conversation that goes along the lines of:

- 'What did you think of the TV film *The Day After*?'
- 'Oh, I never saw it.'
- 'It was reviewed in most papers.'
- 'I never read reviews.'

is not likely to continue for long.

Perhaps this is the reason why many cultures have developed a period of social chit-chat before discussing business. The British can often be found discussing the state of the weather in order to establish this relationship. In most selection interviews it is not normal to pose the most direct, difficult question immediately you meet the candidates unless you want to upset them. For this reason some North American practices are regarded by the British as abrupt.

In my courses where I want to establish teamwork, I attempt to get people communicating with a common objective as soon as possible. The problem occurs at the beginning of the course; if people are strangers there is hardly any conversation. I can get them talking together over work-related issues fairly quickly; it is amazing how soon most start opening up with each other by words and non-verbal communication. However when the coffee break comes there is often a big reduction in this progress because the common ground has been removed. It is now a semi-social occasion. It is necessary to introduce a social topic such as 'What do you think of this part of the country?' or the weather.

We have probably all had reunions with friends and others whom we haven't seen for ages. This usually consists of establishing old memories, shared experiences and testing to see what changes there have been. Conversely, we may have heard somebody say that they haven't anything in common with an old friend any more and that the previous relationship has lapsed. We need some common ground to establish relationships.

Because we are all different individuals, the result of different backgrounds, experiences and learning, we are bound to have different beliefs, attitudes and values. This means that we don't necessarily see eye to eye with everybody, but we need to find something in common for good communication. This can be based on agreement on facts, feelings, attitudes, beliefs or values.

## Tuning in

Assertion and skills in influencing others use these principles of wavelength, understanding and establishing common ground in order to promote good communication. It is the process of crossing the barriers of permitted space between people in order to keep or improve the relationships between them. This is normally done using a combination of verbal and non-verbal skills to tune into their wavelength.

# COMMUNICATION AND MANAGEMENT

Good communication is essential to being a good manager. When we analyse management and leadership activities such as running meetings and speaking at them, interviewing employees for work and at work, briefing, answering questions, checking, supporting, reviewing, delegating, counselling, guiding, resolving conflict, getting co-operation from others, giving and receiving suggestions, agreeing targets and standards, decision making and problem solving, and many other activities, we realise that they are all carried out by communicating. To become more successful managers we need a high degree of skill in communicating.

# 4

# CONVERSATION SKILLS

We may well have found ourselves at one time or another at a loss for words or enduring an embarrassing silence. As discussed in the last chapter, silence can be almost unavoidable if we have no common language or ground. Alternatively, it could be that we did not know how to start and maintain a conversation, even though that was what we wanted to do.

Through spoken conversation we are able to alter and affect the personal distances within relationships. The ability to begin and maintain a conversation with another person, when we want to, is an essential skill of life. It probably seems fundamental to those of us who have no trouble with conversation skills; there are, however, many people to whom this is a great problem. Recent surveys suggest that about one third of British people may be suffering from some form of shyness. We can probably all think of people we know who are relaxed and talkative with others they know well and with friends – probably because they are close and have common language and common ground (wavelength) – but who go quiet when with a relative stranger. There are a number of well-supported 'clinics' now open in London where shy people can learn the skills of starting and holding a satisfactory conversation.

For organisations and, therefore, managers, good communication is vital. With most organisations people are an important, if not the biggest, cost in the budget. Leadership and motivation – which can be defined as getting the best out of employees – should be highly rated. It is achieved through communication with employees (what managers say and do). The manager who cannot converse with his/her employees (as well as colleagues, supervisors and clients) must be at a disadvantage. Even if the conversation revolves around a work objective, it is an asset to be able to build a relationship and establish a co-operative atmosphere. We can probably recognise people who have this skill and, conversely, think of those that we do not relate to or who seem 'distant'.

As managers progress in organisations they become more involved in formal interviews (appointments) and informal talks with others at work. Interviewing has been defined as a conversation with a purpose; indeed, a meeting can be regarded as a group interview. For some senior managers these interviews take up most of their day, and may involve counselling, persuasion, information giving, appraisal, selection, disciplining and listening to or airing grievances. Sometimes they are carried out on the phone. The success of these interviews will be influenced by the way they are conducted and the rapport (mutual wavelength) established.

There are a number of skills in achieving good conversation which are essential to the manager who wants to have a relaxed interview.

# CONVERSATION OPENERS

Conversation openers are statements or questions which give people the chance to engage with others in conversation at a level permitted by their mutual space – to establish common ground.

For people we do not wish to push or pressurise the safest 'opener' is a statement about something obvious, for example a comment about the weather, the season, the number of people present or some other condition that should be recognisable to both parties. It is an attempt to establish common ground at a non-controversial level. It does not necessarily require a verbal response.

If we turn the statement into a question, a response is required. This implies a slightly higher risk of rebuff. If the question is safe, it will normally establish a very basic level of conversation. If the question (or statement) becomes more personal, then the risk of overstepping the other person's permitted space is greater. It depends on the relationship that we have with the person and that each of us wants.

- Low risk statements:
    - 'It's very cold today.'
    - 'It's very warm for this time of year.'
    - 'It's very crowded.'
- Low risk questions:
    - 'It's very cold/warm/crowded isn't it?'
- Higher risk statements:
    - 'It's good to see somebody else here.'
    - 'I'm glad you're here.'
- Higher risk questions:

- 'What are you doing here today?'
- 'What's a nice person like you doing in a place like this?'

Sometimes people feel reluctant to open up on subjects or issues. It is possible to ask a direct probing question, but this runs the risk of being 'nosey' or, again, of overstepping the mark.

- Probing question:
    - 'What exactly are you upset about?'
    - 'Tell me why this affects you so much?'
  may overstep the permitted space limit.

A conversation opener in this situation would give them the option to declare their personal space boundary.

- Statements:
    - 'Sometimes it helps to get it off your chest.'
    - 'I've got time, if you have, to talk about it.'
- Questions:
    - 'Would you like to talk about it?'
    - 'Can I be of any help?'
    - 'Would it help to talk about it?'

The above are sometimes better than direct probing questions because they first establish common ground in that you both have to agree to talk about the subject or issue.

# QUESTIONS

Some interviewers on television programmes quite often ask a two- or three-minute question which can be answered in seconds by one or a few words; you end up by knowing more about the questioner's attitudes, beliefs and values than those of the person being interviewed. Conversely, the politician, by saying 'Before I answer that, let me just say . . .', can deal with the question he/she wanted to answer rather than the question the interviewer asked. This can all be acceptable 'television', where the interviewer is trying to 'corner' or 'trip up' a politician, but may well lead to fight, flight or avoidance (rather than submission). Indeed we are used to disputes between politicians and interviewers and even occasionally to a walk-out.

This principle can be transferred to conversation skills. Good conversation depends on mutual wavelength, understanding and establishing common ground within our permitted spaces. We can review the main types of questions within that light.

## Open questions

- Cannot be answered yes or no.
- The respondent answers in his/her own words.
- Are good for eliciting feelings and attitudes as well as facts and for expanding subjects.
- Are usually prefaced by what, how and why.
  Examples:
    - 'Why did you join the squash club?'
    - 'What do you think about the squash club?'

# Closed questions

- Can be answered yes and no.
- May be used for relaxing a non-talkative person; however, a talkative person may expand, volunteering information.
- May also be used for summarising, classifying or control. Examples:
    - 'So you have joined the squash club?'
    - 'Do you like the squash club?'

# Leading questions

- A closed question that indicates the answer that is required in the mind of the poser.
- Can be used to check an attitude or knowledge or to force a person into an admission. Examples:
    - 'You *don't* think the squash club is good, do you?'
    - 'It's disgraceful that the squash club shuts on Wednesday, isn't it?'
    - 'You spend a lot of time at the squash club; you must really like it, don't you?'

# Specific questions

- For definite information or specific fact.
- Can be used to control the garrulous and clarify information. Examples:

    – 'What year was it when you joined the squash club?'
    – 'Who introduced you to the squash club?'

# Reflective questions

- Reflect back, as a *rephrased* statement, something interesting that somebody has said, usually encouraging the other to expand.
- Can be used to show that you are on the same wavelength, without showing personal bias.
- Are useful where emotions and strong feelings may be involved, to get more depth.
  Examples:
      – '. . . and they made me feel really welcome.'
      – 'So you feel that the squash club takes an interest in new members?'
      – '. . . and I think it is a waste of time and money.'
      – 'So you wish you had never joined the squash club?'

If the aim is to hear and understand properly what a person has to say, the prime question that the good conversationalist uses is the open question. With the right non-verbal communication and listening skills it displays a real interest in what the other person has to say without being too interrogative, biased or dominant.

The reflective question is the second great conversational art and is dealt with under listening skills.

The interviewer who is genuinely interested in another person's real information, attitudes, feelings, values and beliefs will mostly use these two types of question. For the conversationalist (or interviewer) it requires much less thought about what to say and more in the way of listening and picking up information and clues, which will in turn generate their own follow-up questions.

# FREE INFORMATION

Free information is extra to what was specifically asked. The open questioner positively encourages it to be volunteered, whereas we will only get it from a closed question if the other person is talkative, co-operative or both.

A: 'It's cold, isn't it?' (Closed, leading)
B: 'Yes,' (answer) 'but not half as cold as Yorkshire was yesterday.' (Free information)
A: 'Oh, what took you to Yorkshire yesterday?' (Open)
B: 'Well, I have to travel in my job.' (Answer) 'That's why I live North of London.' (Free information)

You now have a choice of follow-up questions:

A: (for the answer): 'Tell me what do you do?' (Open), or
A: (for free information): 'So you live out of London for travelling reasons?' (Reflective), or
A: 'How did you decide where to live?' (Open)

Probably it is better to follow up the free information in this case because it follows the thinking of the other person. We can always return to the first question if it is not answered in the course of the conversation. We are consolidating our position in the permitted space of the respondent and keeping on their wavelength. We are opening up the conversation and therefore the relationship.

# SELF-DISCLOSURE

This is free information about yourself. A two-way conversation can be opened up by volunteering facts and feelings about yourself. If it is on the same wavelength as the other person it shows that you are happy within this level of mutual space and helps the other person to relax. It can identify common ground.

There is a danger however. It may be seen by the other person as an attempt to take over or monopolise the conversation, so it must not be overdone.

A: '. . . So I finally decided to move out of London.'
B: 'Yes, I made the same decision when I moved into Kent.'
  (self-disclosure)
A: 'Really . . . I feel exactly the same way about London traffic
  . . . I used to spend four hours a day driving to and from
  work which used to exhaust me.' (Free information)

If we do not want another person too close to us we 'clam up'. We do not pick up their 'free information' or make any disclosures about ourselves. To do so invites them into our space. On the other hand, if we like the other person we pick up their free information and make disclosures about ourselves which are invitations to a closer relationship — without monopolising the conversation.

# LOOKING AND LISTENING

## Observation

In conversation, the meaning of the words we use is affected strongly by our expressions, gestures and movements, and if we really pay attention to a particular person we usually look at them, whether listening or speaking. For these reasons it is important to maintain eye contact during conversations.

When we are talking, regular eye contact increases the personal impact of our words. Normally if you want somebody to listen to every word you say you increase your eye contact, until for a really important message you are staring at them.

When we are listening, important clues can be gained by watching expression and body language. These cannot be interpreted in a vacuum but depend on the person and situation. The skill is to look for changes in behaviour which can be fairly accurately interpreted with people we know well.

In conversation eye contact generally becomes too low below about 30 per cent while over 60 per cent may become uncomfortable, although, as discussed in the section on non-verbal communication, this depends on factors such as distance, your space and the effect you require. (Non-verbal communication is dealt with in more detail in Chapters 8 and 9.)

# Listening

Because of the nature of words – used as combinations of symbols to express complex images and thoughts – it is important that we concentrate on what other people say if we want to distil *their* meaning. Because we perceive everything through our own experiences, biases and attitudes, it is very difficult:

- To listen to what is said and not said – and its significance.
- To pick up points for later expansion.
- To listen for generalisations and assumptions that may need to be questioned more specifically.
- To pick up the exact expression in a voice. If asked for comments there are many ways of saying 'Oh, not really', all of which convey different meanings.

There is a great tendency to 'listen' to what is going on in our own head and only 'filter-listen' to others. This can consist of only hearing what we want to hear or expect to hear; we listen only to the parts that we can use in our arguments. (Remember the British habit in disputes – *A* against *B*.) We are very aware of (and offended by) the occasions when we feel we have not been 'really listened to' or given a fair hearing.

Detailed techniques of listening are dealt with in the next chapter. What is really important is that listening is one of the greatest conversational skills. It implies not only really trying to understand the meaning of what others say but being seen to be listening.

# MANAGEMENT

Conversation skills are essential to relationships and therefore one of a good manager's abilities. Many managers' success with their staff, other managers and clients is dependent on informal meetings and interviews and establishing a relaxed friendly atmosphere rather than passivity or hostility.

If managers have the ability to:

- open the conversation by establishing common ground
- use mainly open questions
- pick up free information
- use self-disclosure to encourage 'wavelength'
- observe and
- listen to people at work

then they will become known as good communicators.

# 5

# LISTENING SKILLS

Listening is the most underrated skill involved in face-to-face communication – probably because, like reading, we generally regard it as being passive, as compared with speaking and writing which we see as active. Maybe this comes about because, except for a few instances when we really want to concentrate on something that is being said, we usually do not listen very well – we 'filter-listen', which is a process like skimming in reading. Skimming is all very well with a newspaper, which is designed by professional writers to suit the skimmer; it is structured, with headlines, summaries at the start of articles and different sections for different interests. When we filter-listen to someone, hoping to pick out the essential and interesting parts, we are subject to their abilities in spoken expression and our attitudes and biases.

## MEANING AND WAVELENGTH

The art of listening to someone consists of being able to distil the *meaning* from what somebody says. This is much easier if we are on the same wavelength, when words, expressions and phrases usually have the same meaning; for example we are more likely to be on the same wavelength as somebody who is close (space) to us. Listening is more difficult with people with whom we don't have this close relationship. The process of the other person having a thought or feeling, coding it into the words to give us a message, and our decoding the message according to what the words normally mean to us in order to get an impression, is complex. Our society is full of misunderstanding of the spoken word.

- It is common to hear people stating that
    - 'I told you quite clearly', or
    - 'That's what I said', or
    - 'I told you so'
- With others saying:
    - 'You never did', or
    - 'Oh, is that what you said?' or
    - 'Why didn't you make yourself clear?' or
    - 'I don't remember your saying that.'

Effective listening is ensuring that our impression is the same as the thought or feeling that was given expression.

How do we indicate that we are listening to another person? Most people would say it's when you aren't talking – when you are obeying the old command to 'Shut up and listen'. If we add to this correct non-verbal communication we get passive listening.

## PASSIVE LISTENING

This occurs when we remain silent, with our eyes for the most part on the speaker. The eyes indicate our interest in what the person is saying. This is what normally happens to public speakers in meetings when the audience are interested in what is being said. There is a difference when we are engaged in conversation or a form of interview with another person; without any response, the eye contact becomes awkward after a time.

If we get this sort of response when we are talking, unless we are particularly insensitive, we have reactions such as:

- We find the lack of response unencouraging.
- We tend to waffle or repeat ourselves to ensure the message is getting across.
- We find it difficult to keep holding the other person's gaze. A person staring at you most of the time becomes unnerving, as anyone who has played the child's game of staring each other down will know – one of you will have to look away and break the eye contact.
- We find it more difficult to concentrate on what we are saying because we start to wonder what is going on in the listener's mind, to the exclusion of our original message.
- Whereas it puts pressure on us to keep speaking it tends to make us dry up – finishing with remarks like 'Well, that's it', 'That's all then' and other weak endings.

It is also a strain on most listeners not to give any reaction to a speaker over a long period when face to face in conversation. Most of us are not used to talking for two or three minutes or more without interruption. Because the brain automatically relates information it takes in to associated stored information, listeners invariably have facts, thoughts and questions going through their minds which they will want to express.

To summarise, passive listening can be used in groups

but if used one-to-one has the effect of disconcerting the speaker over a prolonged period. It can be used to put pressure on a person but runs the risk that any empathy may disappear from a conversation (wavelength) when the eye contact is judged to be too much for the permitted space. The final drawback is that the speaker does not know whether or not the listener has understood the exact meaning of what was in his/her mind.

## ACKNOWLEDGEMENT RESPONSES

These responses do not noticeably disrupt the speaker's flow; they consist of our saying things or making noises (paralinguistics) to indicate that we have understood the speaker and want them to continue. Appropriate expressions and body movements (kinesics) such as nods, smiles and frowns support the paralinguistics. Thus we respond with such expressions as:

- 'ummmm'
- 'Yes'
- 'I see'
- 'Go on'
- 'mm-hmm'
- 'Really'
- 'Oh, yes'

plus suitable expressions and gestures. These responses certainly have the effect of being more encouraging to the speaker. They make prolonged eye contact more tolerable by making it less of a silent stare.

- Psychologists in the civil service found that interviewers who gave supportive acknowledgement responses to candidates got one-third more information (free information) from candidates with the same questions than passive listeners.

Although there are occasions when passive listening is suitable – in groups, interrogation, negotiation – acknowledgement responses will help the listener promote conversation, especially in one-to-one exchanges.

However, the drawback, of not having any sure way of knowing that the listeners' impression of what was said matches the speaker's intention, is still present. In addition, most of us who listen, trying to understand what somebody is saying, still have our own thoughts, feelings and questions going through our mind, and it is normal behaviour to voice these impressions.

# INTERFERENCE

If we voice our own thoughts, feelings and questions when somebody is speaking to us, we run the risk of not being on the same wavelength. This may lead to communication breaking down. Although it is normal practice to speak your own mind when in conversation with another, it is the reason why listening skills are rarely found, and is the cause of many misunderstandings, misconceptions and poor judgement.

For good communication we need empathy. By overruling someone else's thoughts and words with our own, we interfere with the process of understanding what they intend. We have introduced our own biases and attitudes and this may distort any further communication or lead to a breakdown. It is as serious as radio interference, described in the Concise Oxford Dictionary as the 'fading of received signals by interference of waves from different sources or paths . . . unwanted signals'.

Let us consider the possible results of listeners' comments. If they are not on our wavelength, it will depend on their status (for whatever reason) with us.

> You: '. . . and I don't really get on with them.'
> Listener: '. . . Oh, I find them all right.'
> or '. . . They have always seemed very nice to me.'

This will probably get the reactions, discussed in Chapter 1, of an aggressive or non-assertive response and lead to a breakdown in empathetic communication. It interferes with our wavelength.

Many of our comments and responses when we are listening to someone are more in tune with our own thoughts, feelings and attitudes than those of the speaker. A list of some of these potential barriers to empathetic conversation is given in the following section.

## Interference in empathetic conversation

How judgemental (i.e. critical or supportive) a response is is largely determined by verbal tone and other non-verbal factors.

## Critical responses

This type of response runs the risk that you may feel 'put down' (unless of course you believe that, because of the person's status, they are permitted by you to respond to you like this) and may make you resistant or defensive or inhibit you. Critical responses are thus normally seen as aggressive.

1. *Ordering, directing, commanding*
    - You must do this.
    - Stop it.
2. *Warning, threatening*
    - You had better do this, or else.
    - You had better not try that.
3. *Moralising, preaching*
    - You should do this.
    - You ought to try this.
4. *Judging, blaming*
    - That's not correct.
    - You are not right.
    - You are wrong.
    - It's your fault.
5. *Name calling, ridiculing, shaming*
    - Whatever gave you that idea?
    - I don't know where you dreamt that up.
    - Oh, that's absolutely ridiculous.
    - Tell me another one.
6. *Distracting, diverting, kidding*
    - Think about the positive side.
    - You think you've got problems.

## Supportive sympathetic responses

Responses of this type can miss the mark if they are not what you are looking for from the listener. If you want somebody to understand you and your thoughts this can also make you resistant, defensive or inhibit you. Many research surveys show that the effect of a sympathetic hearing is to put a bias on what the speaker says. So, for example, somebody who is complaining about somebody else and gets sympathetic responses will then exaggerate the wrong they are talking about. They therefore receive very little help in dealing with the problem because they are not talking about the reality.

1. *Reassuring, sympathising, consoling*
   – You'll feel different tomorrow.
   – Oh, I know, it is dreadful.
   – Things are always darkest before the dawn.
   – It might not be as bad as you think.
2. *Praising, buttering up, evaluating*
   – You usually have very good judgement.
   – You've made very good progress.

### Logical analytical responses

These responses can fail because the speaker may not be on the right wavelength to appreciate them. The speaker may find the approach too pushy (into their space). Not many people like cold interrogation, especially if the speaker has been talking about feelings. A logical approach to someone who is angry, for example, is likely to make the person even more angry.

1. *Advising, giving suggestions or solutions*
   – What I think you should do is . . .
   – Let me suggest . . .
2. *Persuading with logic*
   – Experience tells us . . .

    — Do you realise that . . .

3. *Interpreting, analysing, diagnosing*
   - You're saying this because you're angry, paranoid, etc.
   - You have problems with authority.

4. *Probing, questioning, interrogating*
   - Why did you do that?
   - What have you done to try and solve it?

All of these responses may break down the empathy in a conversation and interfere with the communication, thus putting us on a different wavelength.

Even logical-seeming questions can be perceived by the speaker as being too nosey or overstepping the mark, depending on how personal they consider the matter. Implicit in most of the other responses is a judgement, either critical or approving, based on the listeners' own attitudes and values.

Of course these responses may all be considered quite acceptable within some of the relationships we have. They may be permissible within the other person's space and may also suit the situation and expectations of that person.

- You have probably experienced someone putting on a 'helpless act' in order to get a sympathetic response. It is quite acceptable to *them* when they do elicit this reaction, but it can be annoying to *others* who do not want this response when they are talking about problems which they intend to solve themselves.

The real point in calling these responses interference or barriers to good communication is to highlight the fact that, by using them, we run a risk of being on a different wavelength to another person *when* we are *listening* to what they say. They can interfere with the wavelength we build between ourselves and others by establishing differences rather than common ground. We can use them when we are sure that we have understood what they meant, but we will need to check that we have received the correct meaning.

# ACTIVE OR REFLECTIVE LISTENING

Active or reflective listening is a method of responding to people, when they are speaking, in a way that enables us to concentrate on their meaning, without using judgemental or analytical comments and questions. It gives us the best chance of discovering their intention when they communicate with us rather than merely making assumptions about what they mean.

It consists of rephrasing the crucial parts of what someone says to you and returning it to the speaker. It is important to use your own words (based on your understanding of what the person has said) rather than parroting back just what they have said. They are fed back as statements, not questions, keeping you within the person's permitted space.

- e.g. Speaker: '. . . and I don't really get on with them'
  You: '. . . you feel you have little in common'
- e.g. Speaker: '. . . and I don't get on with them at all'
  You: '. . . you feel you have nothing in common'

This form of listening would sound very odd if you did it for everything someone said. It is best used occasionally, along with passive listening and acknowledgement responses. The best occasions to use it are:

- If you are not quite sure what somebody really means.
- If someone has said something with real feeling (emotion) in their voice.
- If someone is talking about their feelings and emotions.
- If someone is talking about a personal matter or problem.

These four situations arise many times in our work and social life. Unfortunately, the 'interference' of criticism, sympathetic and analytic responses are utilised most frequently in these situations — unfortunate in that they are least likely to create empathy (wavelength).

The great advantages of using active listening as a responsive skill are:

- It prevents (or minimises) misunderstanding.
    - It allows the speaker to check the listeners' interpretation of their meaning.
- It shows acceptance of the speaker.
    - It is not critical, sympathetic or analytical but empathetic. If your reflected statement is accurate it shows that you are on the same wavelength as the speaker and have understood what they are saying without being judgemental.
- It defuses emotion.
    - By being empathetic, it helps people feel understood. This calms down their feelings in a way that critical, sympathetic and analytic behaviour cannot achieve.
- It keeps the problem with the speaker.
    - You are not making any attempt to 'take over' and

answer another person's problem, although of course
you always can do so, if invited.

With the active listening technique you are understanding
another's problem and how they feel about it. When this is
done, it is amazing how often this releases the speaker's
ability to solve his/her own problem.

A noted psychologist, Carl Rogers, studied people's
responses in face-to-face communication and found the
following.

- Evaluative or judgemental responses were used most
  frequently.
- Interpretive (based on hunches) responses were used next
  most frequently.
- Supportive (sympathetic) responses were used third most
  frequently.
- Probing (analytical) responses were used fourth most
  frequently.
- Understanding (reflective) responses were used least
  frequently.

These findings will probably be borne out by your own
experiences and underline how rare empathetic listening is
compared with critical, sympathetic or analytic listening.

I recently came across active listening referred to in
North American books and research and realised it was a
well-proven technique which had been used in Britain for
years by many psychoanalysts and psychotherapists to help
people solve their own problems. A practitioner called
Maier called it reflecting technique and published ten
guidelines.

1. The interviewer should reflect the respondent's feelings in his/her own words rather than serve as a mimic or parrot.
2. Remarks should be prefaced by:

   You feel . . .

   You think . . .

   It seems to you that . . .

   although later in the interview these prefaces should be dropped.
3. Reflected remarks should be formulated as statements and not as questions.
4. It is important to wait out pauses. The respondent may be trying to sort out his/her thoughts and may be on the verge of expressing them when the interviewer breaks in with a question or remark.
5. When many feelings are expressed, only the last one should be reflected.
6. Only feelings actually expressed should be reflected. It is dangerous for the interviewer to start guessing at feelings he/she thinks may be there.
7. When inconsistent feelings are expressed the interviewer should proceed as if no inconsistency had taken place.
8. If a person cries during an interview, the interviewer may refer to the fact so long as the respondent is not trying to hide the tears.
9. Decisions, solutions and constructive ideas may be reflected when these predominate over feelings of confusion, hostility, fear, insecurity, rejection, etc.
10. In reflecting another state of mind, any indication of approval or disapproval is to be avoided.

In any face-to-face spoken communication, effective listening must be accorded an important place. In social conversation the ability to be 'a good listener' is a great asset; it is astounding how often a good listener is called 'a good conversationalist'. How much more vital it is at work where problems need to be understood before they can be solved and ideas need to be taken in before they can be evaluated.

Reflective listening is an active skill and of essential value in assertiveness and in influencing others. It is the ability to be able to listen in a way that does not risk your rejection by getting within another's space, and improves wavelength between you so that the relationship can improve. It is a single skill that can change a person's perceived behaviour enormously with others.

## LISTENING AND MANAGEMENT

A manager is commonly defined as someone who has to get work done through other people. This must imply a two-way communication with senior management, colleagues and subordinates. Listening, reading and looking must be half the communication equation. If I were asked what is the single criticism or lack of ability perceived by most subordinates, it is that their management do not listen properly – that is, with understanding. In nearly every list of qualities of a good leader, under some guise or other is found the ability to listen with understanding. There are many managers who have managed to hear what people say but have not tried to understand the other person. Check your own experience and see whether you have always been listened to by management.

The manager who wants to be a good communicator must add to conversation skills the ability to use: –

- acknowledgement responses to encourage others to talk and
- reflective or active listening, especially when others' problems, ideas and emotions are being expressed.

Listening is perhaps the easiest skill of life to put into practice, but is the one least encountered. Many people who have started to use it have found that not only have people's attitudes towards them changed dramatically for the better, but they have also become able to see others as individuals with whom they can relate.

# 6

# PERSUASION SKILLS

The ability to persuade others to see and agree with our point of view is one of the most highly valued communication skills. The need for this skill is well recognised for salesmen and saleswomen, who are hardly ever asked to do their job without some sales (persuasion) training. Even temporary door-to-door salespeople, such as students selling encyclopaedias, are given a crash course. In some organisations a great section of the training budget and time goes on sales training.

However it is not only salespeople who have to use persuasion skills. Managers are nearly always trying to persuade someone or some group to take some attitude or action. Certainly at meetings persuasion skills are essential for managers who want to influence decisions. The way to check how often we try to persuade others is to ask if there is a resulting action that we want as a result of our communication. We may inform or explain in order to persuade; it is the objective, which is more than giving information or understanding to others, that makes it persuasion. A manager may hold a meeting to inform employees of company results and to explain them, but if it is done in order to get co-operation with future plans then it is persuasion.

Persuasion skills can be crucial to the success of management activities such as:

- gaining employee acceptance and agreement
- negotiating
- introducing changes
- implementing plans
- gaining recognition of their section's work, products or services
- co-operation with colleagues and senior management
- relations with clients
- planning and agreeing budgets

## MAKING YOUR POINT

The most important skill in making your point is to be brief, effective and relevant. There is a great tendency to show care and concern for a subject by enlarging on it and finding as many arguments as you can. This shows research and knowledge but obscures the point you are making by hiding it among many subsidiary facts.

Harold Macmillan, later to become Prime Minister, was congratulated on his maiden speech in the House of Commons by David Lloyd George (the then Prime Minister), but reports that Lloyd George told him that he couldn't remember any of it. Asked why, Lloyd George said 'Too many points'. The advice was to stick to one point in a short speech in order to make it memorable and therefore effective.

In a lecture lasting over half an hour we probably need to make notes if we want to recall what was said. If we rely on memory we may be able to distil the main point(s) but are more likely to remember only those things that interested us. Similarly, listening to another person's report of a film, play or game, can often make us think that it was completely different from the one that we just witnessed.

At work there is an even worse habit – that of trying to emphasise that work has been done by mentioning or listing every fact and detail, regardless of whether it has any significant bearing on the main point or not. This is the same as 'padding out' school essays to make them conform to a required length.

- A public inquiry into a proposal for a nuclear power plant is nearing its conclusion. Five tons of paper have been used in reports and more than seven million words spoken. Who can hear, read and remember such a mass of detail? Perhaps the main points are being lost.
- This pales into insignificance compared to a session of the United Nations General Assembly which generated 5663 tons of paper.
- I took a temporary job when I was a student, as a 'bouncer' in a discothèque and later in a night club. I was soon taught by the experienced 'bouncers' (those who got their way without violence or starting a fight) that if you wanted people to comply, you did not get into arguments, but just stated your wishes (demands) very simply and stuck to them – a way of working which leads us to an assertive skill.

## BROKEN RECORD

In the same way as a damaged record can repeat over and over again the same phrase, so we can stick to our point.

This can perhaps be best illustrated by determined door-to-door salespeople.

- You may well say 'No, I'm not interested in encyclopaedias', etc., but the persistent salesperson is trained never to take no for an answer. They will take another line of attack, trying to establish mutual ground such as 'Are you interested in your children getting a good and complete education?' The only defence is to be equally persistent and not get distracted by side arguments.
- e.g. Caller: 'Are you interested in education?'
  You: 'Yes, but I'm not interested in buying encyclopaedias.'
  Caller: 'Do you have children?'
  You: 'Yes, but I'm not interested in buying encyclopaedias.'
  Caller: 'Are you satisfied with the standard of education for your children?'
  You: 'Maybe, but I'm not interested in buying encyclopaedias.'

  Until your message gets across.

Again, if you are trying to put a case you will often get responses which do not answer you. Politicians are often expert at evading questions in this way. It is a matter of 'sticking to your guns' or persisting with your questions. Many of us have been fobbed off with half answers and diversions. The skill of knowing what we want to say, saying and repeating it when it is not effective is an integral part of assertion in everyday social and business life.

To be really effective, in the long run, we have to use this 'broken record' technique without getting emotional. We need to gear all our non-verbal communication to making ourselves appear reasonable, calm and composed. This technique of avoiding manipulative verbal traps, argumentative baiting and irrelevant logic by calm repetition is dealt with later on in more detail (combined with other techniques) when we come to using our skills to cope with difficult situations.

It is of great use when:

- we are in conflict
- refusing unreasonable requests
- asking questions for clarification
- correcting someone who has higher status
- expressing feelings or values especially when the other person is not listening

It is an essential skill if you want to protect your own space and not let others diminish you by taking advantage of you.

# PERSUASION SKILLS AND ATTITUDES

There are many times when we want to introduce a new idea to others or to change their minds about something they know. Alongside the non-verbal skills there are three basic approaches which can be chosen, depending on your judgement of their attitude towards the idea.

## Direct

This stresses the advantages of your recommendations and the disadvantages of other options, although we must avoid terms like 'I'm right and you're wrong' which are aggressive. The direct technique is best used when you know the recipient is open to or might favour your proposal; it is good for the genuinely open mind and for people who will receive it well. It states the facts.

- **e.g.** This car has a better reliability record than your present one according to all independent reports.
- **e.g.** If you smoke regularly when you're aged twenty there is a 50 per cent certainty that you will never see sixty.
- **e.g.** We must invest money now, to take the great opportunity that this proposition offers us.

## Oblique

The oblique approach gives credence to other options but brings out the facts against them. It can seem natural because of its apparent 'even-handedness'. It is best used when people may be slightly cynical or opposed to new ideas or change. When others say they have an 'open' mind this is often what they mean – they need a lot of persuasion to change their views. It avoids the direct sales pitch, which can often arouse suspicion or resistance. It anticipates the opposition arguments by dealing with them.

- **e.g.** Mark Antony's speech after the death of Caesar (in Shakespeare's *Julius Caesar*). When he addresses the citizens who are 'for' Brutus because he 'has rid Rome of a tyrant' he uses such persuasion as:
  'Yet Brutus says he was ambitious;
  And Brutus is an honourable man.
  You all did see that on the Lupercal
  I thrice presented him a kingly crown,

Which he did thrice refuse. Was this ambition?
Yet Brutus says he was ambitious;
And, sure, he is an honourable man.'
(N.B. Remember his good 'conversation opener'
establishing wavelength: 'Friends, Romans,
countrymen, lend me your ears . . .')

- e.g. Many of you may like to smoke for your nerves. It's a
  good reason . . . of course, it means that half of you
  will never see sixty – but you'll be less nervous about
  it.

- e.g. Many people will say this is not the right time to be
  investing money. I would normally be the first to
  agree with them (wavelength), but if we examine this
  great opportunity we shall see that in the long
  term . . .

# Converse

The converse approach puts the 'other' argument in such a
way that it is bound to be rejected. It apparently favours
the option that you don't want in order to bring home the
weaknesses. It is best used when you know that you have
stubborn opposition, you would not get anywhere with a
direct approach and even a seemingly fair (oblique) approach
would be likely to fail because of bias.

- e.g. I heard a great converse talk by an artificial grass
  salesman to some football managers who were all
  against artificial pitches. He started by saying: 'Most
  of you know me and expect me to give you a sales
  talk for our range of artificial pitches. I'm not going
  to do that – I want to talk about a new surface that

has come to my attention.' He then proceeded to talk about this new surface which retained water, froze, churned up, gave variable bounce to the ball, etc. It took quite a time for the managers, saying 'this is rubbish', to realise that he was talking about grass pitches. He may not have sold his product that time but he certainly made the managers think again.

- e.g. 'It's a free world. If people want to smoke, let them. It is their business that they will suffer chronic illnesses, fill our hospitals and that half of them won't live to see sixty . . .'

- e.g. 'This isn't a time to be spending money. The proposition is that we would get lasting benefits, but the facts of life at the moment are that we can't speculate with money no matter what the return.'

It is all a matter of assessing your listeners and choosing the line that is best. If there is going to be a discussion (with other views) it is best to anticipate any opposition that is likely to arise before it does. This weakens the opposition argument because you have already considered it and may even prevent it arising in some cases. It is the same technique as looking for the strengths in another practice (*A* against *B*).

## Give evidence

It is always better to give listeners information instead of opinion. Many people can be swayed by knowledge of where your facts originated as well as by what you say and how you say it.

It is worth quoting highly credible sources of authority

whenever you can to support your case. If the status of your source has authority it can gain the same acceptability as experience in changing people's attitudes. However, if it is overdone or the source is not accepted you can provoke rejection, sometimes just out of contrariness.

## Illustrate your point

One of the key ways of helping someone to understand your point is to illustrate it with an example. It is especially useful if you are making a general principle or summarising facts. If the example is on the same wavelength as the other person it becomes especially powerful and difficult to refute. It is no accident that Jesus Christ used parables to illustrate his teachings in terms his followers would understand – 'The Good Samaritan', 'The Lost Sheep', vineyard owners, etc.

As an example, which would you be persuaded by if you were buying a car? Someone talking about the maker's statistics for petrol consumption or someone telling you how many miles per gallon they got out of their last trip? General points need examples to make them come to life. John Garnett, former Director of the Industrial Society, always says that you use the example to prove the rule! The skill is to use a vivid example to illustrate your main point, not to scatter information and stories evenly. Think about the only thing you want people to remember and illustrate it.

# SUMMARY

If we can combine these skills of:

- keeping our persuasion brief
- keeping to one or a few main points
- persisting (not being diverted)
- supporting our evidence with acceptable sources
- illustrating our main points
- and taking account of attitudes (anticipating opposition)

we shall be numbered among those people who are regarded as persuasive. This is a skill that makes managers stand out in organisations. They are the ones most likely to get their budget demands, results and satisfied employees.

# 7

# COPING WITH CRITICISM

In this chapter 'criticism' is used in the sense of censure rather than judgement or review, either of which can be favourable as well as adverse.

Managers find that they spend a lot of their time persuading when they are communicating, and for this reason they are likely to attract criticism. It is the process outlined in Chapter 2 where *A* looks for the weaknesses in *B*'s case and vice versa. The process can continue to identify other weaknesses from previous experience and even to get personal.

There is a body of thought that holds that the best decisions are the product of disagreement. Peter Drucker wrote in his book *The Practice of Management* that 'The first rule in decision making is that one does not make a decision unless there is disagreement'. Robert Townsend, former Chairman of Avis Rent-a-Car Corporation, says in his book *Up The Organisation* that there is a 'sure fire way of rating your new idea. If everybody gives it something between active indifference and hot opposition the idea is valid. Also the importance of the idea will be directly proportional to the amount of passionate opposition it stirs up.'

# COPING WITH CRITICISM AND OPPOSITION

Even if we are very good at making our point and persuading people we are bound to encounter opposition and criticism. Indeed, some people say that if you have these skills, it is almost inevitable. There is certainly much evidence that success attracts criticism whereas lack of it invites obscurity. Let us look at the skills of dealing with these responses.

## Opposition to your ideas

The opposition is not personal, but based on your arguments and proposals.

- The key to this skill is to seem reasonable and allow the other person to save face. Remember *A* against *B* in Chapter 2.

## Anticipate the opposition

Of course, a persuasive person has anticipated the opposition by taking account of it in his/her original case. Despite this, the criticism will still arise. If we want to avoid a direct attack, which will get the traditional response of aggression or non-assertive resentment, we have to find some way in which they can change their views without diminishing their status (a climb-down). We have to preserve both our space and the other person's.

# Saving face

To save face you must find something you can agree with in the other person's argument. This makes you seem reasonable to other people and takes the aggressive sting out of any counter-arguments you may make, without diminishing their weight. It makes your counter-attack more acceptable to others. To be effective, though, it must be genuine.

We are probably all familiar with a version of this technique which is so overused it has now lost its meaning and is often a warning signal to others. How often do you hear someone say:

- 'With respect' before mild disagreement, or
- 'With the greatest respect' before greater disagreement.

Introductions of this type have become commonplace because people have found they worked well in the past. Now, however, they are so transparent that they may even draw groans from the victim or be ignored. They often have a reverse effect when they are perceived to be false.

Other versions are less used and have far more power:

- Agreeing in principle. 'As a general rule you're right . . .'
- Agree with part. 'Of course, you are absolutely right that . . .'
- Admit it is a reasonable argument. 'What you say is very logical and I'm sure that many would agree with you . . .'
- Raise objections as an afterthought. 'Yes, that seems true . . . but if . . .'

- State your wish to agree if you could. 'I can see your point and it's a good one . . .'

Whatever you agree with has to *be* sincere and to *sound* sincere! This is the technique of finding the strengths in another's case (*A* against *B*).

## Appeal to self-interest

Any subsequent argument after the type of face-saving statement given above can be strengthened by using an appeal to self-interest. You have to think of how the person in opposition likes to think of himself and add it to the argument.

- Caring person '. . . but I am sure that we managers – who care about the welfare of our staff – would take the line that . . .'
  '. . . but I know that – as people who have the needs of the people at heart – we have to . . .'
- Thrifty '. . . but I am certain that we – who believe in getting value for money – will take the line that . . .'
- Intelligent '. . . but – all of us here who value common sense over emotional feelings – will see.'
  '. . . but if we take the logical course of action then . . .'

Such responses, if delivered in a reasonable voice, will make it very difficult for anyone to return to the attack without seeming uncaring, a spendthrift or unintelligent – unless they deal with these implications. If they do that they appear more aggressive and less reasonable by seeming personal. You are appealing to their known needs so that your solution may satisfy them.

# PERSONAL CRITICISM

I don't know anybody who likes criticism, especially if it is personal. To a certain extent *all* criticism is personal and therefore aggressive because we own and identify with our ideas and logic.

I have often met people who, at first, said they 'did not mind constructive criticism'. When they were questioned, however, it transpired that what they meant was that they didn't like being criticised, but sometimes they could see the justice in it and sometimes admitted they were wrong and changed their behaviour as a result.

The problem with this response to criticism is that for most of us it represents a climb-down or some loss of status. What we need are methods of coping with personal criticism that do not involve the loss of self-esteem.

## Fogging

Fogging allows you to receive personal criticism without becoming defensive or anxious. Remember A against B in Chapter 2. It involves you calmly acknowledging possible truth in the criticism without confirming that it is right or wrong. It gives no reward to manipulative criticism or nagging, while keeping what empathy there may be. The skill defuses the confrontation so that you apparently accept the criticism without a definite or aggressive response and enables the critic to maintain face. Neither loses status, this being the basis of assertive skills.

What you do is to:

- Agree with any truth in the criticism
  **e.g.** 'Yes, I am often late . . .'
- Agree with the possibility, however slight
  **e.g.** 'Yes, I could very well have been late myself . . .'
- Agree with logic
  **e.g.** 'Yes, I can see why you think that I am inconsiderate . . .'
- Allow for improvement
  **e.g.** 'Yes, I could probably make a bigger effort to get here on time . . .
  'Yes, perhaps I could do it better . . .'
- Empathy
  **e.g.** 'Yes, well I can understand your feeling that way . . .'
  'Yes, that's a good point . . .'

What you are doing is offering no resistance (aggressive or defensive) so that they find it very difficult to continue. Your non-verbal communication is 'calm and collected'. You acknowledge any part of the criticism that you can agree with, and wherever possible you empathise with the other person's point of view. You are hearing and trying to understand their point of view, thus making it easier for them to hear yours.

## Negative assertion

Negative assertion enables you to acknowledge personal criticism without loss of status. You accept that you have made an error or have a fault, without apologising, seeking forgiveness, trying to make up for it, being defensive or aggressive. You calmly accept the real mistake with comfortable non-verbal communication. This technique again removes the grounds that the critic is using.

The advantages of doing this are that you retain your dignity and can feel comfortable with yourself while respecting the other person's dignity and status. You maintain your space. The technique is to:

- Agree with criticism:
    - 'Yes, I do lose my head when I get excited.'
    - 'Yes, I sometimes am moody.'
    - 'Yes, I told you the wrong date.'
    - 'Yes, I forgot the keys.'
- Agree with the critic's value system:
    - 'Yes, I should have done that better.'
    - 'Yes, I really could have tried harder.'
    - 'Yes, it is a bit stupid to say that to him.'

Many people find this very difficult to do because of their early environmental programming and social conditioning. A lot of people have guilt feelings built into them or a habit of never admitting mistakes.

In political history there are many figures who have achieved notoriety by trying to deny accusations which have later proved to be correct, President Nixon being one of the most infamous examples. In contrast, it is very difficult to remember people who resigned at the first sign of suspicion with an admission that they might be at fault.

In the same way fogging and negative assertion take away the grounds for aggression without losing dignity or status in social situations. There are, of course, legal situations where they would not be the best responses, in that they imply partial or complete admission, and there are, equally, situations where you would want to take a more positive line.

# Negative enquiry

The negative enquiry probes the negative aspects of personal criticism in order to get more information. You actively prompt the critic for reasons which enable you to get the real information or exhaust it. It also gets the critic to be assertive and less dependent on manipulative ploys.

Many people offer personal criticism that is generalised and not wholly based on factual evidence – you question it in a calm way (non-verbal communication, NVC).

- e.g. Critic: 'I think you aren't being fair to others.'
    You: 'Could you tell me in exactly what way you think I'm not being fair to anybody else?'
- e.g. Critic: 'You really have been very "stand-offish" lately.'
    You: 'Oh, can you tell me in what way I've been acting like that?'

The technique enables you to ask for the evidence behind a critical statement so that you can resolve the matter. Often criticism is the result of relationships and feelings and the original statement is just an indication of this. To unearth the real reason may require quite a bit of delving by negative enquiries.

- e.g. Critic: 'I think you always ignore people's feelings.'
     You: 'Really, could you tell me why, in particular, you say this?' (calm and reasonable NVC)
     Critic: 'Certainly, you didn't listen to anybody this morning at our meeting.'
     You: 'Oh! – perhaps you could tell me when you noticed me not listening.'
     Critic: 'Well, I felt you had missed my point when I tried to talk about my ideas on the new parking arrangements.'

Now you can try and resolve the specific problem rather than dealing with general criticism. Sometimes by using this technique, the criticism dissolves as it is shown to be unfounded or too petty to deal with. It also stops people trying to manipulate you.

It is an especially useful technique for people who are quite close to you in relationships. By using a low key unemotional approach you treat the criticism seriously and do not damage the relationship.

# SUMMARY

In any organisation there will be people who see things differently from you. They have different ideas, goals, standards and experiences. This leads to open conflict in aggressive organisations and, at the least, to unpleasant innuendo in non-assertive organisations. The manager who can cope with this, seem reasonable and retain his/her self-esteem and rights, is usually the person who will influence the unbiased.

Genuinely used techniques of:

- anticipating the opposition
- saving people's face when you disagree
- appealing to self-interest
- fogging
- negative assertion
- negative enquiry

will make you more assertive. You are protecting your own personal space while respecting that of others.

# 8

# MORE THAN WORDS

Non-verbal communication plays an important part in assertiveness and skill in influencing others. In this and the following two chapters we examine the elements of non-verbal communication – vocals, body language, surroundings and positioning. In reality, of course, all the elements are intermixed to create the total impression. Status, for example, can be conveyed by voice, expression, gesture, posture, distance, height, dress, etc., usually in combination.

I have often encountered great resistance when discussing non-verbal communication, possibly because analysing what we usually react to intuitively and instinctively seems to destroy a certain mystique. Possibly, as psychologist Albert Mehrabiam said, it is like trying 'to put a rainbow in a bottle'.

What *is* known is that the effect of face-to-face communication comes largely from non-verbal rather than verbal communication – meaning is not so much in the words, which can be written down, but in voice, expression, gestures and movements of the speaker. These factors can affect not only the meaning of the words but also whether the listener feels liked or disliked.

Mehrabiam even went so far as to propose a formula for how the listener drives the effect of a spoken message:

- 7 per cent words or verbal (what is said)
- 38 per cent vocal (how it is said)
- 55 per cent facial expression, movement, gesture

A message is really powerful if all these elements support each other. However, the acid test is not the scientific validity of these figures but what happens if these elements are in conflict.

We have already discussed how we can change the literal (verbal) meaning of spoken messages by using our voice. With sarcasm we can change the words to mean the opposite. If someone calls you 'Darling' in a cutting tone of voice, you are likely to feel disliked; it is not what you say but the way that you say it that is important.

What happens if we are confronted with conflict between the verbal/voice message and actions, gestures and expressions? We certainly doubt the message and the sincerity of the speaker. If somebody says 'I love you', however warmly, without any supportive expression and movement, the message loses most of its impact and meaning. We even react to people who don't 'smile with their eyes'. We can conclude that actions speak louder than words.

## Vocals

Vocals include all the sounds and noises we can make with our voice, apart from the words themselves – the intonation, volume, projection, pitch, stress, emotion, speed and pauses which give and change the meaning of our words.

# THE WORDS WE USE

Words themselves obviously still carry some meaning, apart from the obvious translation. We can sense the tone of a letter or notice, but by altering the words, even though the message is the same, we can make written communication more friendly, interested and personal or more hostile, disinterested and official.

We have different types of words that we use for different occasions; we may almost change our vocabulary in different circumstances. For most people this can be seen in the way they speak one language but write using a different set of words. At the extreme we can say:

- 'The door's over there to your right'

and write:

- 'The access/egress point is located adjacent to the point of convergence of the northern and eastern facets of the accommodation.'

We can talk with a person in an informal language and later hear them using very formal language in an official meeting.

We use more distant forms of words rather than simple, immediate or direct ones when we find communicating the message is undesirable or uncomfortable. This can be caused by the message itself or by the relationship with the other person. So the words:

- 'That proposal is considered inappropriate, at this moment in time' is more distant and unfriendly than:

- 'We don't consider this idea is suitable at present'

which is more distant than:

- 'We've thought about your idea, but don't think that we can use it right now.'

# FRIENDLINESS

Communications in 'officialese' are less friendly than a more personal style. Just think how informal you are with people you like compared to others you don't know. You may become still more formal when there is a difficult message to convey. For example, in close relationships, the use of the diminutive or pet name might be replaced by the full first name for an awkward message.

Some organisations with a formal communication style can seem unfriendly and unsympathetic to the public because of the language they use. Many organisations have therefore changed their images by evolving a more informal or personal communication style.

Friendliness or other feelings for people can also be detected from people's voices, regardless of the words. We only have to think of the way we convey our feelings and permitted space when we talk, sometimes unintelligibly, to babies and animals. Experiments using electronic filters which render the words unintelligible but leave the vocal qualities intact get significant agreement on the degree of friendliness conveyed by certain uses of the voice.

# USING THE VOICE FOR MEANING

Most people are expert at injecting their feelings into their words by the use of their vocal abilities. This skill is so inbuilt with most of us that it needs little conscious thought when talking to people in order to convey the impression that we want. If we really feel pleased to see someone, it merely requires conscious programming of our subconscious skills to express this pleasure in our voice (remembering that a direct immediate personal message is more friendly than a formal one).

We should be aware that if we are to derive the full advantages of speaking over writing then we can add meaning to or subtract meaning from our words by the skilful use of our voice. For example, the trade union or management negotiator can make a possibly outrageous statement or demand seem more reasonably by using measured unemotional tones. Listen to debates in the House of Commons, the Trades Union Congress and other such forums, and you will clearly hear the advantages to be gained from the ability to convey feelings or play down emotions.

This section on non-verbal communication also covers all the vocal sounds and noises we make which are not connected with words – sighs, groans, ums, ers, ahs and gasps. These really show our power to express our feelings and liking for people without words.

Using the sound 'mmmmm – mmmm', we can change its meaning from dislike to warning, from neutrality to liking. We can express an enormous variety of feelings just by sounds without words . . . fatigue, boredom, liking of a person, amazement, disappointment, sadness . . . the list is virtually endless.

In terms of relating to our space and others' feelings, our voice and vocals play a vital part in establishing permitted and wanted distance. The fact that by talking we can convey, exaggerate or conceal our feelings not only about what we say but also about another person is very important in our ability to assert ourselves and influence others.

## MANAGEMENT, WORDS AND VOCALS

The implications of this chapter affect managers in two important ways.

First it demonstrates that the words a manager uses to communicate give recipients a direct guide to the relationship that is sought. By changing the words of a memorandum to employees, for example from long abstract, less-used words to more familiar, easy, concrete ones, the manager can change the whole impression by making the message friendly. (It must similarly be realised that the opposite reaction will be elicited by a 'starchy' formal letter or a notice full of officialese.) Such letters and notices may be inviting friendly co-operation but will probably get the opposite response. There are examples of strikes being triggered by the 'tone' of such letters and notices.

We must also be aware that the implicit tone of the words we use can be too friendly to suit one of our normal relationships. An example of this is when people receive personalised letters in their junk mail (unsolicited sales letters) and object because their first name is used through-out the letter by an organisation that they do not know (and probably do not want to know). The words are overstepping the permitted space limit.

In contrast, if we use long formal words we can make a statement sound more official. This can add weight to a communication if it suits the occasion. It can be amusing, though, to note some of the words found in communiqués during strike negotiation, such as 'exacerbate', 'on-going situation', 'intransigence' and 'at this moment in time' especially when used by people we suspect would not normally use them. There was once a story that Henry Kissinger, the American politician, had found that too many people were saying 'at this moment in time' so had changed his version to 'at this juncture of maturity'.

The second implication of this chapter for managers is that the spoken message can often have less effect than the way in which it is said. Points can be lost not only because they are obscured in the text but also because they are not emphasised by the voice and timing. For example, the use of pauses can have a dramatic effect on the impact of a message. One of the greatest handicaps for someone trying to persuade others orally is not to sound enthusiastic. When managers are speaking with employees, their friendliness and sincerity can be gauged from the tone of voice. Additionally, the impression they produce can be reinforced or contradicted by the use they make of body movement, expression and gesture – and these are the subjects of our next chapter.

# 9

# BODY MOVEMENT, EXPRESSION AND GESTURES

This chapter deals with what is popularly known as 'body language'. As we have seen, if it is in conflict with what we say we tend not to believe the words. Tests with posture and relaxation show that they are good indicators of attitude and status towards another person. We usually incline towards people we like not only with our feelings but also with our bodies. However, it is important not to make assumptions when trying to read this form of non-verbal communication but to pick up pointers and judge them in context alongside other types of communication.

It is also useful to know the normal physical behaviour of the other person. If we think of somebody we know well, we can probably think of the tell-tale indicators they may make for different feelings, like anger, tiredness, happiness, etc., such as:

- forehead-wiping for tiredness
- face-touching for anxiety
- scratching for self-blame
- fist-clenching for aggression or tension
- finger-wagging for dominance (invading another's space?)

Seated people who suddenly start to kick a foot may be indicating that they don't like or don't agree with what we say. However, it may equally well be caused by thinking of something disagreeable, or by anxiety about the time; it might be a childhood habit, or simply that they have got 'pins and needles' or their foot has 'gone to sleep'! It can still be used as an indicator of something – the important thing is to pick up sudden changes in expression or behaviour.

There are many books which deal with this subject in detail, even with national differences. We can consider only a few indicators here which are useful in conversation skills. These indicators can be voluntary or involuntary, depending on how consciously we make the expression or gesture, but they are present in all communication.

# SMILING

There are probably no words, gestures or feelings expressed in the voice that convey liking and interest as much as smiling. Of course there are many types of smile, but the genuine one is an indication of acceptance and often an invitation to get closer to another person in terms of psychological space. This is why salespeople often use this powerful non-verbal communication, even when they don't like it. It is a vital ingredient of making others welcome when we meet them. However, the artificial or 'fixed' smile is counter-productive. It is often detected because it is not reinforced by other non-verbal signals, and probably gives rise to the saying 'Beware of those who smile too much.'

Most of us smile involuntarily when we see something that we like – as I write this now, I am smiling because my cat has jumped up on the desk and is trying to get my attention by sitting on my writing paper, batting my pen with his paws and rubbing his head against my nose.

- I can remember a woman who gave a talk to a lot of people who thought they were fairly expert on the subject. The atmosphere was almost hostile at the start, but the woman showed genuine interest and concern (though possibly not genuine liking!) for the audience by her non-verbal communication, particularly smiling. It wasn't long before the atmosphere changed and the audience were mostly smiling back.
- Another memory I have is of being criticised by a person after my session on a speaking course. His voice was reasonable and he smiled to show real interest in me. I responded by smiling back and nodding agreement with what he said. It certainly helped me to allow him to say very personal things to me without violating my permitted space. I permitted him to say things that, from others, would most likely have offended me.

## HEAD NODS

If we think about influencing skills, we mostly think of getting others to see things our way or agree with us. Often when we are putting our case we don't actually want others to interrupt but merely to give responses by non-verbal communication such as the head nod.

There are various meanings to head nods in Britain (besides meaning that somebody is falling asleep). The single head nod is often taken for agreement. This can be a mistaken assumption, because if the paralinguistics

AH-HUH! or Mmmmmmmh! are added to the nod, it really only means that the person is following our argument. They may well wish to disagree later with all or part of our case. It implies permission to keep on speaking, and as such is a useful gesture in listening.

The double (or multiple) head nod is far more likely to indicate positive agreement. Again, if we add the typical paralinguistics such as Yes, Yep, Right, Yer, Yah, Sure, Mmm, we can detect the difference.

Fast multiple head nods usually imply more than agreement. This normally occurs when whatever we have said has sparked off a relevant memory in the other person. This means that we can invite the other person to support our case with a good degree of confidence.

Recognition of these non-verbal signals can be of great use if we are in conversation, negotiation and other types of interview or meeting.

## EYE CONTACT

Our eyes are very expressive — as some say 'the windows of the soul!' — so it is worth examining two aspects of this factor in communication.

As previously discussed, we increase eye contact if we want to give a message impact, if we want to 'get it across' to someone. Increased eye contact is also a good indicator of someone who is paying attention to us.

In the same way as we look more at objects that interest us and less at something that we dislike, so we behave with other people. We actually avert our eyes from things that disgust us . . . unless of course we are fascinated! Similarly we often mistrust people who cannot hold our gaze, calling them 'shifty'. Somebody who wants a child really to listen to them may well say 'Look at me when I am speaking to you!'

Eye contact not only shows the importance we attach to what we or another person is saying; it also conveys our interest in, or liking for, another person. The interest may be generated by a desire to dominate the other person or catch them out at something (which is aggressive), although increased eye contact is usually associated with liking for the person or positive interest in what he/she is saying.

If an expert raconteur is holding forth, it is normal for everybody to have their eyes riveted on that person. If somebody is very close (or wants to be very close) to somebody else you can usually detect frequent glances between them when they are in a group as they check the other's reactions, even if somebody else is talking. In a business environment this may happen because the accepted power of a person in a group generates the interest. It is usually fairly easy to detect the leader of a group, whether appointed or real, by the direction of eye contacts, regardless of the speaker.

The lesson to be learnt from this is to suit our eye contact to what we are saying and to our relationships. If we address a group without looking at them we are psychologically insulting them. On the dramatic stage it is a general rule not to turn your back on the audience; without eye contact we reduce the impact of what we say. Looking at all of them equally conveys not only that we are talking to them individually, but that (with the supporting body language such as smiling) we are interested in them.

Many of us are familiar with the situation of conversing with somebody, with good eye contact, when another person joins in. If the person we were talking with then starts giving all their eye contact to the other person, we may make attempts to get it back, or lose interest because we are being ignored. It is a psychological insult often denoting status; it distances us in terms of space.

We can increase our eye contact when:

- we want to add impact to our words
- we want to show that we are listening
- we want to show interest in what they are saying
- we want to show that we like the person

However, like smiling, if it is artificially overdone it can produce an adverse reaction. We must remember our 'permitted space' – we can tolerate longer eye contact with people who are close to us, but tend to look away from strangers. It is rude to 'stare'.

The other point about eye contact is mostly subconscious. It concerns pupil dilation. Perhaps a story will best illustrate the point. On a television programme several male members of the audience were selected to assist in an experiment. Identical twin women were introduced who had been given different harmless drugs, one to increase eye pupil dilation, one to decrease it. The men were then asked to make a choice of which woman they preferred. Of course, being British, the men said they were both equal in their eyes, but, on being pressed, they all chose the woman with the dilated eye pupils.

The message from this is not sexual, but simply that we increase our pupil size when looking at something that interests us or that we like. The men were not conscious of the reason for their choice but were responding to a subconscious reaction which is in all of us; we cannot normally consciously control our pupil dilation. Because of this, some American advertisers have found it more accurate to measure pupil dilation rather than use machines with 'like/dislike' buttons with test audiences when they are previewing their possible commercials.

This means that with eye contact we can be giving or receiving messages from the pupils which may contradict or support all the other behaviour. Perhaps this explains why some people, when all the other signals are supportive, are still not trusted. If their pupils contract it may indicate that they are not happy with the person they are talking to, or their message. This can be a factor when considering the advantages and disadvantages of wearing spectacles; certainly it can sometimes be uncomfortable to deal with someone who wears dark glasses, in that we may feel at a disadvantage, and rightly.

Sales and many confidence boosting courses have tried to overcome this reaction by encouraging people to 'think positively'. Indeed modern sales training tells you that, if you dislike a person, you should try and concentrate on the only positive thing you can think about them, such as the way they dress, in an attempt to control your non-verbal communication.

# GESTURE CLUSTERS

The study of gesture clusters demonstrates combinations of non-verbal communications give us our impressions of others and shows how much of it reflects our attitudes towards others. It is not enough merely to analyse single items such as eyebrow movement, for example:

- fully raised – disbelief
- half-raised – surprise
- normal – no comment
- half lowered – puzzled
- lowered – angry

To gain any insight we must view these aspects of non-verbal communication in conjunction with others.

Gesture clusters give us an impression:

- Open and sincere
    - open hands
    - moving closer
    - leaning forward
    - uncrossed arms and legs
    - easy long eye contact
    - smiling mouth
- Defensive
    - clenched hands
    - maintaining or increasing distance
    - leaning away, curling up
    - arms and legs tightly crossed
    - minimum eye contact, darting eyes, looking away and
      down
    - lips pursed

but this non-verbal communication has to be viewed in context with all the other factors such as the message, paralinguistics, surroundings and positioning. This last element is covered in the next chapter.

# 10

# SURROUNDINGS AND POSITIONING

In this chapter the various surroundings and positions we can find ourselves in when communicating with others are discussed. This is probably the most neglected section of non-verbal communication in training, although we all have some knowledge of it. Again, it is probably easier to discuss the subject in sections, although in reality it should be perceived in conjunction with all the other communication factors.

## DISTANCE AND TOUCHING

When we looked at territorial space, we considered how we position ourselves at different distances from others to suit our relationships. I also mentioned that this varies by nationality; southern and Latin races have much closer distances for each category of relationship than those from the north. We only have to look at traditional public greetings in different countries to see that the British are usually very distant and 'cold' in their relationships. Latin races have a variety of behaviours for welcoming and meeting someone, including embracing and kissing them on the cheeks, while the North Americans shake hands, grab arms and put arms over shoulders. Even a Northern European race such as the Germans shake hands normally on meeting and leaving each other. The British, in contrast, will shake hands only on formal occasions and certainly embrace only family and very good close friends in public. There has been many a person in Britain left with their hand half-extended and ignored, or rather embarrassed and hesitant about whether to offer their hand.

If we reflect further we can see that this maintenance of physical distance by the British is suggested by their tendency to maintain greater psychological distances than many other races: the reluctance to show emotion in public or 'make a scene'; the typical British understatement often used after a particularly harrowing experience; the British 'stiff upper lip' and 'sang-froid' under pressure.

From the point of view of assertion and ability to influence, the closer we are to somebody, the more we can influence them. We close up (even with the wagging finger sometimes) if we want to add impact to our words. It is easier to ignore a 'distant' message. Certainly training courses become more personal if the tutors can reduce the distance between themselves and the participants. If we want to have a close understanding with someone we try to arrange a 'tête-à-tête' (literally head-to-head) with them, although again we have to remember that getting inside a person's permitted space can have an adverse reaction. There is a film of a Canadian reception for Arab diplomats which shows the Arabian delegates closing up on the Canadians to get their correct distance and the Canadians backing off to preserve theirs. Speeded up it looks almost like dancing.

The act of touching another person (not aggressively) is associated with interest and liking, and can be illustrated by an interesting experiment that involved a group of librarians and the public.

• The librarians attempted to touch a certain number of their clients casually, for example brushing their hand with theirs. When the clients were asked what they thought of their librarians, most said that they thought they were 'caring' and 'understanding' people. With the clients they didn't touch at all the reaction was different; they just elicited comments like 'They do their job, I do mine.'

This is why it is an advantage for a salesperson to shake hands when meeting a prospective client and to reduce the distance between themselves within the permitted limits. In contrast, the traditional image of the lord and lady breakfasting at opposite ends of a long dining-room table conjures up the thought of very stilted, formal conversation.

Distance and touching are not only governed by our national habits and relationships with others but can be used by us to help create the effect and relationship which we desire. Think about where you would plan to sit at a meal with others if there was someone there with whom you wanted a closer relationship.

## BARRIERS

Barriers are furniture or other physical obstacles which we may find between ourselves and a person with whom we are communicating. They have the effect of increasing distance. It is possible to be very close to a clerk at a booking office or bank, but if there is a perspex screen or grill between you, you cannot get within their permitted space at all; you can be ignored even though you are within their normal permitted distance and would usually attract instant attention. Such communication is often very formal, lacking in warmth and impersonal.

The greater the size and height of barriers, the greater is the effect of distance between people. A low coffee table is less of a barrier than a large solid desk. The traditional 'classroom', with people at tables or desks in rows, gives those at the back the most distance, not only in terms of real space but also by reason of the barriers caused by those in front of them. We are probably all used to lecture halls filling up, with most people sitting at the back or the edges, a position which gives them the security of being protected by a wall, if not behind them, at least to the side. They thus have less personal contact with the lecturer and are relatively safe from invasion of their space.

There is a police textbook which recommends that, for interrogation, the interrogator should sit close to the suspect with no desk or table between them, 'since an obstruction of any sort affords the subject a certain degree of relief and confidence not otherwise obtainable'. The police officer starts by sitting down about two or three feet away, 'but after the interrogation is under way, the interrogator should move his chair in closer so that ultimately one of the subject's knees is just about in between the interrogator's two knees'. This is an invasion of the respondent's permitted space and is designed to put him/her under such pressure that he or she finds it difficult to resist or lie.

We can all think of interviews where the questioners sit comfortably behind large desks or tables and the applicant is made to sit in the open and is meant to relax!

- Which table would you choose in an empty restaurant? Probably not right in the middle. The most favoured position is one with your back to the wall (protected) from which you can see all others.

# ORIENTATION

We normally lean forwards or incline our whole bodies towards somebody who interests us, although this does not always mean liking – we could just as easily be trying to dominate someone. We can consider three distinct positions and the possible reasons that cause them.

## Side by side

Side-by-side orientation usually denotes unity, alliance or at least neutrality between people. It is normal to 'side' with people of like views. This position, however, does not always encourage communication. It is common to see two people, often friends, or married, sitting in silence side by side (with their backs to the wall) looking at others but not speaking. (Of course you can still have good communication with someone at your side; this is dealt with in the section below on the third position.) This position is represented by:

# Face to face

The face-to-face position is the one we adopt when we want to add impact to our communication – it increases direct eye contact. We might arrange such a position for an intimate dinner for two, when we would sit closely opposite our partner so that we could easily engage his/her attention and eye contact.

We also normally adopt this position when we want to be aggressive or dominate others. The traditional management/union position is 'across the table' and 'eyeball to eyeball'. It certainly increases the pressure on another person by being direct and very difficult to avoid; it is not the normal communicating position unless people are naturally very close in their relationships (permitted space). It can be represented:

the position of confrontation.

# At right angles

Orientation at right angles is the normal relaxed position for communication. Have you noticed how people position themselves for a casual friendly conversation which nobody dominates? It is in a circle. 'Circle' is a name given to participative groups and it is no accident that when management and unions wish to have a reasonable discussion and arrive at an agreement, they talk about 'getting round the table'.

It has the effect of enabling a good amount of eye contact, within a fixed distance, without becoming embarrassing and without allowing anyone involved to take up a position of dominance. If two people are having a comfortable conversation, even if they are sitting side by side, they will assume a body orientation that can be represented as:

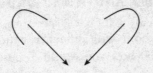

You will notice, however, that if a point of dispute comes up, one person will move to confront the other, may well close the distance between them and will often bring out the 'six-shooter' of conversation, the wagging or pointing finger.

## Effects

The effect of moving towards face-to-face position is to decrease the space between people and increase the effect of eye contact.

If you sit side by side without much eye contact, it is possible to sit very close to each other. Often delegations who sit like this at the negotiating table retire to have a real discussion, positioned differently, before answering a proposition. Close ranks signify unity but don't normally promote communication, apart from the shouting of slogans in unison.

If you are at right angles to a person, you can get fairly

close without it becoming uncomfortable for either of you. However, if you then turn to be face to face you will notice a difference in your personal territory and space. It makes the distance seem much less, although physically it may be the same. The effect of increasing eye contact by orientation is of great importance in non-verbal communication.

## ROOMS AND HOME GROUND

The nature of a room will influence your communication and space. Consider how you would discuss a problem with a person:

- in a grand cathedral
- in a formal court room
- in a public house
- in the favourite room of your own house

Generally our space is influenced by the following factors:

- The higher the ceiling, the more hushed the tones.
- The more formal the room, e.g. oak panelled, the more you are stilted and formal.
- The larger the room, the more quietly you speak – unless of course it is crowded, with a high noise level.
- The more familiar the room, the more you are normal and relaxed.

There is a lot of evidence to show that, by holding a meeting in a different venue, the whole nature of the communication can change. Those involved in training know that it can make the difference between failure and success.

The point about home ground is well known; we all become more on our guard and defensive in strange places. If we can pick our own ground it has a great effect in our social and business lives. The discomfort that we feel on being invited into a person's home where we don't know people is reflected in the boss who says 'Step into my office' rather than coming out to see us. However, we must remember that although we may be happy on our home ground, it does have an effect on others. Although we are more likely (according to evidence) to get our own way on home ground, there is sometimes a case for giving away 'home advantage' or looking for neutral territory.

## DRESS

Dress doesn't fit easily into any of my arbitrary categories of non-verbal communication but is none the less a major factor in communication and relationships.

There is no doubt that we dress to identify with groups; if we join groups, unless we want to be noticed as different, we conform to their standards. All groups have 'norms' or standards and attitudes about this; this means that we tend to judge each other by our dress. It is all very much to do with wavelength.

- A group of betting shop area managers I was training were judged as 'snooty' and formal by a group of solicitors in the same hotel. My group were wearing suits and the legal people casual clothes. The reality was very different, but because of their dress my group was almost restrained while the solicitors were 'letting their hair down'.

There is no doubt that if we are the only person dressed differently, or if we think our dress does not match up to others present – unless this is intentional – we feel uncomfortable. This will affect our ability to relax and communicate with others, and will usually affect their communication with us. The work interview (not necessarily a selection interview) is a good example of a situation in which this factor can affect assertion skills and ability to influence others.

## STATUS

Status is a product of all the non-verbal and verbal communication factors; however, it is, as defined by dictionaries, related to position. The British have for centuries been programmed to recognise status in a form called 'class'.

## Status and stature

In a recent experiment a stranger was introduced to different groups of students, in turn, as an interested party, a postgraduate student and as an expert professor. His height was guessed, respectively, by the different groups as less, about the same and greater than his real height. Stature was thus related to status.

When we hear someone talking with a person or about them, we can usually assess the person's status; the paralinguistics indicate respect or lack of it.

- My wife was amazed when she met one of my great
  student heroes – the great Van den Berg. Her comment

after hearing all my stories about him, was 'But he's smaller than you!' My reply was 'Not in my eyes'. I 'looked up' to him and held him in 'high esteem' and respect.

Probably you have experienced the same thing when you have heard friends talk about a stranger. We can certainly pick up a person's status from the presenter when we are introduced to him/her for the first time. The problem is that we may be taking in so much non-verbal communication and assessing them ourselves that we may forget their name – a great status destroyer.

## Names and status

How do you react when someone gets your name wrong or can't remember it? Our name is something that is built into us – probably the only thing left of importance when we die! It is necessary for people's self-respect that you remember their names. If people are good at this skill they will be remembered and admired themselves, thus giving them status. The best system is really to listen to the name and not to the mass of other information and thoughts that are going through your mind at the time of introduction. Then, use the name frequently in conversation; like all repetition, there is some hope of it sticking and it makes conversation more personal.

If you wish to improve on this, there are simple memory systems, some based on association, that can help us remember people's names. If we can remember and use a person's name we give ourselves more chance of being on their wavelength; if we don't, then we diminish them and ourselves, thus risking a breakdown in communication. Diminishing yourself detracts from your status.

## Using height

We can add to our status artificially; as it is connected with height, so we can affect it by adjusting our physical position. Methods of doing this are discussed later but, put simply, changing status by changing surroundings and position is very much to do with level. Normally if we stand and the other person sits we have the advantage of status. People with bulk or 'presence' can also create this effect, as can very tall people.

## Relative position

Status is not totally concerned with height, but also with relative position.

- When as an RAF officer I heard charges against offenders I sat at my desk with my cap on. The airman on the charge was marched in formally without his cap and made to stand at a distance from me. I had the definite advantage through non-verbal communication, even though I was at a lower level.

Normally greater status is associated with greater height, especially if it is the biggest chair (and the most favourable protected position). Did King Arthur at his round (good for communication) table have the biggest chair? Where does the chairperson sit – protected at the back, with the window/light behind them so they can see all others? We only have to think of the formal High Court to think of status.

- All have to stand when the judge comes into the room.
- The judge(s) sit in a dominant position, higher than others (except sometimes an unruly public gallery!).
- They wear different dress – wigs and gowns to give them status.
- The accused is made to stand for formal address.
- The layout is such that the eye contact and, therefore, control is designed to be with the judge at crucial moments.
- The prosecution/defence counsel wear wigs and gowns to denote their status, even though they may be physically lower than the accused.
- Formal address is used to the judge.

We can make similar arrangements concerning status.

- We can stand above a seated audience, thus helping us to dominate.
- We can stand below seated people, as in a lecture room, with raised tiers of seats to focus attention on ourselves.
- We can be on a rostrum or stage, seated above an audience.

In business the following are common.

- We can keep someone waiting till we are ready.
- We can give them a seat away from the protection of our desk or keep them standing.
- We can make certain we are on our own territory, in the

favoured position with the light behind us, walls round us and the other person in the middle of the room on a smaller chair.

Of course, the position can be reversed by a determined person. It only needs someone, when invited to take a seat, to say,

- 'No, thank you, I'd rather stand for what I've got to say!'

to reverse the process.

The important point about status, surroundings and positioning is to get to the same level if we want good communication. This is usually expressed in sayings like:

- 'Seeing eye to eye'
- 'On the level'
- 'I'll level with you'
- 'Standing up for your rights'
- 'I'm going to stand up to him/her'
- 'I'll bring him/her down/cut them down to size'

although the last two are more usually associated with attempts at aggression or dominance.

Status is very much connected with wavelength, assertion and influencing skills and can, in conjunction with other verbal and non-verbal skills, be used to great effect. As it is the product of more than surroundings and positioning, it is worth while to consider how you can use all your non-verbal communication to achieve the effect you want.

# DEALING WITH OTHERS

## Introduction

To appear friendly to others it is useful to smile, shake their hand if possible, remember and use their names, take an open stance, oriented at right angles at a distance you and they appear happy with. Support conversation which arises from your open questions with head nods and acknowledgement responses such as Uh-Uh, Yes, I see. Keep frequent eye contact.

## Meeting people you know and like

Appear and sound really pleased to see them. It is amazing how often the British can greet someone they know and like with a very off-hand 'Oh, hello there' accompanied by an almost deadpan expression. It is the result of years of not showing emotions in public.

## Relaxation and status

Home, away or neutral ground can be chosen, depending on whether you want yourself, them or both of you to be relaxed.

Home ground, together with status ploys and distance, can put you in a position where you are more likely to get your own way.

- I was told by a training officer for the Citizens' Advice Bureau that she encouraged her staff to interview people on the same side of the desk, oriented at right angles. She said this got people to open up far more about their real problems. They felt that they were not just dealing with another official but somebody on their wavelength who was interested in what they had to say.

- I was once asked for advice because management and union consultative meetings in an organisation had deteriorated to a point where there was no goodwill left. I found out that the management used one of 'their' rooms, went in first, sat side by side with their backs to the far window and walls. The unions came in second and sat side by side with their backs to the space of the room. My initial recommendation that they intermixed was agreed by both sides. They later said that this simple change had affected their meetings radically and, although they still had problems, there was much greater mutual co-operation and less political 'siding'.

- There is no doubt that Lord Carrington had greater success in achieving majority rule in what was Rhodesia and is now Zimbabwe than Ivor Richard. It may have been the product of the situation but there were also some different non-verbal tactics. Ivor Richard first tried to get all the parties to a neutral venue in Geneva. For status reasons the negotiations were to be held round a large round table. However, some parties challenged his status, saying they wanted a minister of the crown to conduct the meeting. The round table was done away with and finally Mr Richard held the meeting in a formal manner which gave him more status by the use of distance. The meeting eventually finished with not much progress and a second meeting could not be reconvened until Lord Carrington's in London. In contrast, Lord Carrington chose a large house in London (home ground), gave himself the same advantage of status by distance but added to it by being in the most favoured part of the room in a bigger chair and on an elevation. It was interesting that after he had got agreement for the new constitution of Zimbabwe some of the other parties were heard to say that although they had agreed, Lord Carrington had exerted pressure on them.

# IMPROVING OUR NON-VERBAL COMMUNICATION SKILLS

If you study non-verbal tactics at work or socially, you will be surprised (if you were not aware of it before) how many people use them as an aid to achieving their objectives, often seemingly unconsciously.

We do this all our lives but most of us are unaware of our skills and therefore do not try to develop them. We seem to pick up a range of skills, such as nodding to encourage others to speak, that we are not conscious of. What we *can* do is become more aware of our own and others' reactions to our non-verbal communication, so that we can modify our behaviour to get the response we desire.

Many managers consciously use non-verbal skills in order to affect their communication with others. As it has so much effect on their communication, which is an essential part of their job, I would say that all managers or would-be managers need never be bored when people are about; it is usually a first-class chance to watch others and their reactions to non-verbal factors.

## PART THREE

# USING SKILLS ASSERTIVELY

# 11

# HANDLING COMMON MANAGEMENT PROBLEMS

In this chapter we discuss how to deal with some common management problems in an assertive way.

## SAYING NO

Some of us do not have a problem with saying no, or, if we do say yes, have no problem being appreciated for it. It is other people who get 'lumbered', who are easy to manipulate, but who get very few thanks for their efforts. There is a common saying among social and work groups: 'It's always the same people (volunteers) who do the work.'

Now, I don't advocate saying no beyond the point of unreasonableness; this would be aggressive and unco-operative, and would offend other people who would soon distance themselves (space) from the responder. Saying no most of the time doesn't establish wavelength between people and will strain a relationship. What we need is the skill to be able to say no when we are within our rights and it is our choice, and the ability to do it in such a way as not to change our relationship with the asker.

For those people who have non-assertive behaviour this

can be very difficult. There can be any number of reasons
for the behaviour:

- a desire for a quiet life
- it avoids trouble
- it seems friendly and co-operative
- they have been programmed (children, school, church,
  work) by rewards to regard obedience (accommodation) as
  good behaviour
- they like to conform

It means that they often can be made to agree to things
that they would rather refuse.

## The assertive way

The technique of refusing people when we are within our
rights can combine some of the skills we have already
discussed.

- 'broken record'
- non-verbal communication
- wavelength
- reflective listening
- self-disclosure
- free information
- saving face
- fogging
- negative assertion

Broken record is the key to saying no. With a cool, relaxed
voice and other suitable non-verbal communication you

calmly repeat your refusal. You focus on that intention and refuse to be sidetracked.

This can still be hard to do with a very manipulative person who plays on your values (e.g., loyalty, friendship), emotions and feelings (e.g., they may cry or get angry). Sometimes we can be made to feel that our refusal will damage our relationship. This is where we can combine the broken record technique with the others to keep our wavelength while we persist.

- ● e.g. Self-disclosure (information about yourself):
  - – 'I'm sure I would feel very much as you do, but I cannot agree because I have made previous arrangements.'
- ● e.g. Free information (acknowledging their reasons given to you):
  - – 'Well, I can see that this is going to put you and your family out, but, all the same, I have a previous arrangement.'
- ● e.g. Saving face:
  - – 'Well, you have put a very strong argument, but I really have to stick to my arrangements.'
  - – 'I can see why you see it as you do, but I really have to stick to my arrangements.'
  - – 'I can well accept why you think it's important that I should do what you want, but I know it is more important that I stick to the arrangements I have made.'
- ● e.g. Fogging:
  - – 'You may well be right that I'm being selfish this time, but I have got to stick to my arrangements.'

        – 'Yes, I probably seem very stubborn and disloyal but
           I think it is reasonable in this case because of my
           previous arrangements.'

- e.g.   Negative assertion:
        – 'Well, you are right to say that I haven't done
           anything to help you so far, but I must really keep
           faith with my other arrangements this time.'
        – 'Yes, I agree that I am being difficult and unhelpful
           but I think my previous arrangements justify my
           attitude.'

If emotion is used against us, then the best thing is to use reflective listening. This calms the emotional side of the brain by trying to understand people's feelings (empathy) and release the analytical side of their thinking.

- *Other* (angry): 'You never do anything to help me when I need you – you're never willing to do anything when you're wanted!'
  *You* (resisting all temptations to attack – calm and relaxed): 'So you feel I don't try to help you.'
  *Other*: 'Well, it's really that I need you to help me this time.'
  *You* (resisting all temptation to say how often you have helped and that trivial things are always being presented as urgent): 'I can see that you would like me to help but I have really got something I have arranged which is far more urgent.'

If you don't like this response, think what you would say . . . and who to. You can probably go over a few similar situations in your mind, thinking of how you would have liked to use one of these responses.

By now you should be equipped to deal with unwanted door-to-door callers.

- 'Yes, I understand that you would like to talk to me about double glazing/encyclopedias/religion, etc., but I am really not interested.'
- 'Yes, I can see that you have a lot of evidence to support your case, but I am really not interested.'
- 'Yes, I am sure that you feel I have nothing to lose by talking about it, but I am really not interested.'

And so on. You are standing up for your rights while treating the other person as a human with rights. This is assertiveness.

If we practise saying no we eventually find that there is no reason (apart from our early programming) to feel guilty about saying no to people. We can then use the skill in many different business situations.

- 'Well, I can see why you say I don't care about the staff, but I cannot give you a day off tomorrow for the reasons I have given you.'
- 'Yes, I should have told you before about the arrangements, but it still means that I can't give you a day off tomorrow.'
- 'I probably should have checked with management before now, but you are still on the second shift.'
- 'I can understand why you think it is important to do it your way, but I have to insist that you obey safety regulations.'

## Leadership

The important point is not whether you would ever say exactly these words – we must use our normal common language – but whether we are treating the other person as a person with rights, status and dignity, even though we are saying no. Relationships at work are the key to communication, effort, morale and productivity; how we treat people affects these factors. We work more willingly and with more effort for some people (whom we respect) than for others (who usually don't respect us).

The problem for some managers (accommodating) is that they find it very difficult to refuse or deny their employees, colleagues and managers. If they are to co-ordinate their individuals into a team then there will be many occasions when they will have to say no to unreasonable requests. There will also be occasions when the manager wishes to correct an employee although no request has been made.

## CORRECTING OTHERS

'Tact is the ability to make a point without making an enemy.'

Anon

There are many occasions in our social and business life when we find the need to try to correct other people's behaviour.

- We can think of examples in social life:
    - 'Oh, don't do that, it will annoy the neighbours' or

  – '*Please* – I'm trying to concentrate' or
  – 'You really ought to show more consideration for
    others with the way you leave things.'

- Probably all of us who have worked have had something
  we have written changed by somebody else. They justify
  their action in crossing out what we have written with
  words like:

  – 'It will read better this way,' or
  – 'Oh – don't write that! – that will get completely the
    wrong reaction.'

These are not usually serious corrections to another person's
behaviour, but they run the risk of developing into a
'British way of argument'. Such situations are the result of
the understandable reactions of people to little things that
others do that they do not agree with. The problem is that
people often try to correct others in ways that do not bring
the relationship together, simply because they use methods
which can be described as interference; they show that they
are not on the same wavelength as the other person by
implying that they know better. This may well be true, but
it is not welcomed by the other person!

- Are you happy, even if people are right, when they tell
  you to 'turn the volume down' when you are listening to
  some programme or music? Still worse – how do you react
  if they just turn it down without speaking to you?
- Think about how you feel when somebody corrects your
  writing at work and changes your words.

It is amazing how many serious arguments develop from
trivial matters such as which end you squeeze the toothpaste
tube or whether you put the cap back on; whether you have

your desk tidy or untidy; whether you clean the basin or bath after you; whether or not you keep to minor work arrangements, no matter whether you do your job well or not.

'Personality clashes' at work are often built on such minor 'faults' in behaviour or views. By using the techniques in this section of the book it is often (not always!) easy to resolve these differences.

The great secret is no secret; it is to stay within your own rights while respecting those of the other person. Our own feelings or thoughts are within our rights and we are completely justified in stating them if another person's actions do not coincide with them. If we can put them into words that do not condemn the other person or offend them in a personal way (aggression) then we are combining the two great assets of tact and honesty. We give the other person a fair chance to change their behaviour voluntarily, without 'loss of face'.

The attempt to correct somebody else should be phrased so as to indicate clearly that we are conveying our own feelings or thoughts:

- e.g. 'I think that . . .'
  'I feel that . . .'

We should follow this by a non-judgemental description of the behaviour. Non-judgemental means that we do not show approval or disapproval of the other person's action:

- e.g. 'If you play the music at that volume . . .'
  *not* 'If you are going to be so inconsiderate . . .'

- **e.g.** 'If you write that . . .'
  *not* 'If you "put them down" like that . . .'

The last part of our message is to give a good, honest reason why they should change their behaviour.

- **e.g.** 'Our neighbours will come round complaining like they did last time.'
- **e.g.** 'They may well feel offended.'

These examples demonstrate a change of emphasis, from criticism and telling people what to do to being honest about feelings and thoughts and giving people a good reason to change their behaviour, without imposing a solution on them. This technique allows the other person to see our point of view, without our being aggressive, and gives them the chance to put the matter right themselves. If the other person responds with a suggestion that suits us then, by being honest and open (assertive), we have achieved all we wanted without causing offence by being critical (aggressive).

Such a solution has all the advantages of 'accepted' over 'imposed' discipline, in that people are more committed to suggestions they have made themselves. It also allows them to learn; they are given a chance to correct themselves which can bolster their skill and confidence in being able to avoid a repetition of the actions or views that we did not agree with.

- **e.g.** 'I feel that if you use the words "futile" and "insist" in your letter Mr Y will think you are being aggressive and trying to "put him down".'

- **e.g.** 'I think that if you present your prepared proposals to your staff meeting they will react badly because they will think they haven't been consulted.'
- **e.g.** 'I feel if you don't tell them how much you are interested in their proposal they will feel you have lost interest. They may well look for somebody else.'

This is a relatively simple skill – but think back; if someone at work has tried to correct you recently how was it done? If you were correcting someone else how did you do it? Was it a case of saying 'Don't do this, do that?'

The change in style, from imposing a solution to outlining the problem and suggesting reasons for trying to find a solution, is from aggression to assertion. In the ideal situation the other person will appreciate your point and volunteer an action as a solution. If this meets your needs, then you have achieved satisfaction and the other person may also be pleased with having thought of the solution. This feeling can encourage them to be independent and self-correcting.

There are many people who openly or covertly resent being told what to do, especially if it involves a change in their behaviour. We may have heard people say, 'If you want other people to do anything, ask them to do the opposite.' Using assertiveness improves your chance of achieving collaboration without damaging relationships.

## DEALING WITH REACTIONS

Even if we do use an assertive technique for correcting people, we can still receive an unfavourable or aggressive reaction, although we must remember that this would probably have occurred if we had used any other technique. Using the assertive technique, at least we have given the other person a chance to offer an acceptable solution. If we have the power, then we can always try more aggressive methods if the first approach fails.

- **e.g.** 'Well, I'm going to insist that you turn the volume down.'
- **e.g.** 'All right – I am sorry but I am not going to let that letter go out like that. You must change those words.'

Whereas we can go from assertive to aggressive if the need arises, it is very difficult to change the other way. This is because we have moved off the other person's wavelength by invading their permitted psychological space and it will be difficult to resume a normal relationship. Techniques of dealing with defensive (aggressive) responses are detailed in the next chapter.

If we give an assertive message to try and correct another person, rather than giving a solution or an aggressive response the other person may ask us what we want them to do – they may ask for advice. This allows us to make our suggestion without being aggressive. We do not invade their psychological space because, by asking us for advice or suggestions, they have permitted us within it.

- e.g. A: 'I feel that if you say that their behaviour is "intolerable" they will think that you are being aggressive and you will not get the co-operation you want from them.'
  
  B: 'Oh, you may be right . . . What would you say instead?'

> A: 'Well you could try saying that their behaviour is causing you financial difficulty with your cash-flow and you cannot maintain the contract on the present basis.'

- e.g. A: 'I think that if you present your proposals at the beginning of the meeting, they will think that you don't want to get their ideas and suggestions.'

> B: 'Well, that wasn't what I intended — how would you do it?'

> A: 'Maybe you could outline the problem again, and then listen to their ideas and comments. They may well come up with your ideas — but then you will have the advantage that they have suggested them themselves. You can summarise their ideas and add your own suggestions to the debate afterwards. It is still your decision, but they will feel that they have been fully consulted. Of course, when you tell them your decision you will have to give them your reasons, especially if you don't agree with them.'

## COMMON GROUND AND WAVELENGTH

A different situation arises when we do not have a close relationship and we want to correct somebody's behaviour or views. In this case it may be a good idea to establish common ground. This puts you both on the same wavelength within your relationship and can prevent misunderstanding. We can also anticipate opposition by this tactic.

- e.g. 'I know you are in a rush in the morning and have to get to work early, but I feel . . .'

- **e.g.** 'I appreciate all the hard work and effort you have put into this report but I think . . .'
- **e.g.** 'I know you really do want ideas from your staff and you do encourage and listen to them, but I think . . .'

If they are to work, such attempts to agree common ground, of course, have to be honest and accepted by both parties.

# THE MESSAGE

The whole message may now be given as:

- **e.g.** 'I appreciate your love of rock music, but if you play it at that volume we will get the neighbours round complaining again or even, as they threatened, phoning the police . . .'
- **e.g.** 'I know you are very busy, but I think that if you don't telephone Mr X today he will think that you don't want his business.'
- **e.g.** 'I understand your feelings about that firm, but if you write to them saying "we must demand" I think they will feel we are putting too much pressure on them and may move their business elsewhere.'

Most people will say that an essential ingredient in good relationships is mutual respect. Indeed, in management it is one of the requirements that people on leadership courses usually say is essential. Respect is not a quality that people themselves possess, but rather something that others give to a person. People to whom we give respect have more authority with us.

The way respect is gained and developed is by giving

respect to others, by being honest and open (assertive) but by not overstepping the mark (aggressive). This technique of not putting people down when correcting them but of looking for collaboration allows you to build mutual respect.

There are times, however, when this simple method may not suffice, when we are correcting not a minor matter but something more serious.

# 12

# CHANGING PEOPLE'S BEHAVIOUR AT WORK

For many of us the most difficult communication skill is the ability to change another person's behaviour or attitude rather than merely correcting it. Of course if the other person gives us great status we have a good chance of doing it, but to try it assertively, protecting our rights and space and respecting that of others, is difficult. We come back to the typical British reaction to poor food or service in a restaurant, or the typical British manager and the substandard subordinate in Chapter 1 on 'Behaviour and Effects.'

In order to get their way, most people react with non-assertive behaviour: they avoid the problem or try to accommodate it (hinting at their solution or putting it in a way that can be ignored). Alternatively they resort to aggression. Some people change from one reaction to another. They suffer in silence until it becomes too much and then erupt in aggression, startling or hurting the recipient.

There are problems with both these types of behaviour. The non-assertive approach has no guarantee of being willingly accepted because it is seen as criticism which can be ignored, if it is voiced at all. The aggressive approach may get compliance, but not always willingly. It stirs up resentment and counter aggression. Most people don't like solutions that are imposed on them. As the famous inventor Sir Barnes Wallis said in almost his last recorded words – 'You know, if I have discovered anything in my life, it is that people don't like ideas that they haven't thought of themselves.'

# THE ASSERTIVE MESSAGE

We should only use an assertive message if the matter is worth bothering about and we cannot solve the problem by another, more normal form of message or behaviour. If this is the case, how can we confront people in an open and honest way which enables us and them to retain mutual self-esteem and relationships? It is a combination of many of the skills we have already discussed.

In order to keep the relationship intact, the message should be in the normal language we use with the other person, thus preserving our wavelength. Nobody can give us more than an idea of what to say to somebody else; we must use the words that we are happy with and that we know the other person understands.

There are four essential elements to such a message and two optional ones (British version) if we want to use an assertive message to change somebody's behaviour.

## Use 'I' Not 'You'

If we are trying to change someone's behaviour or attitudes, then it will usually be received as criticism and, as it is personal, as personal criticism. This will normally get a defensive or aggressive response.

Most criticism is offensive because it oversteps a person's permitted psychological space. This happens when a person exceeds their rights with someone else by making them feel guilty, blamed, put down or rejected. They react by showing a lack of respect and non-acceptance, which leads to a loss of status if it is accepted. This is not the best atmosphere in which to achieve change.

The main factor causing this effect is the use of the word 'You' . . . at the beginning of the message:

- e.g. 'You should do that better.'
  'You made a mess of that.'

The alternative is to say 'I', thus keeping our message within our rights. We can speak for ourselves but have no 'right' to change another person. We can speak openly, honestly and directly to someone if we speak our own mind rather than preface the message with the manipulative 'you'.

Another reason for saying 'I' is because, if we want someone to change their behaviour or attitude, it is *our* problem. Whether they are happy with their ideas and actions or not, they have chosen them. This causes *us* the problem because we wish to do something about it. By prefacing the message with 'I', we acknowledge that it is our problem.

## Best reason

Establishing the best reason for particular behaviour, in order to show understanding and establish wavelength, is something that can be done with British people. It also anticipates possible opposition.

- e.g. 'I know you have a lot of demands on your time . . .'
       'I realise that you like to get back quickly to see your
       family . . .'

Of course, if we cannot think of any such reason, then we can omit this part of the message.

We include this 'best reason' because it makes our message more acceptable; without it the assertive message seems abrupt and aggressive.

The best reason must be true, not merely false praise which starts the message off with dishonest manipulation. At the worst it must be what the receiver believes to be true. We thus establish common ground and can level (status) with them.

- e.g. 'I know you are very busy.'
       'I am aware that you have been putting in long hours'
       (only if this is true!)

## Feelings

The next ingredient of the assertive confrontation message is the statement of our feelings. This part of the message is essential as it is the part which compels people to consider our request to change.

In order to distinguish between this and manipulative use of emotions, the feeling must be absolutely genuine. (If we don't feel strongly enough about the behaviour, why try to change it – it is obviously not much of a problem to us.)

The technique is:

- •        to state feelings honestly
- •   *not*   state the effects, e.g. surprise may lead to anger if a young child bursts a paper bag by your ear, but the original feeling was great shock
- •   *not*   be judgemental (using the effects)
  -    **e.g.**   'I know that you are very busy but I am very upset that . . .'
  -    *not*   'I know that you are very busy but I am disgusted that . . .' (This is judgemental, implying a value as a result of the emotion or feeling.)
  -    **so**   'I am angry' is a feeling, but 'I am very disappointed with you' or 'I am furious with you' or 'I feel abused' are judgemental
- •   *not*   make a British understatement
  -    **e.g.**   'I am rather disturbed'
  -    **or**   'I am a little perturbed'
- •   *not*   to transfer feelings
  -    **e.g.**   'The management is annoyed . . .'
  -       'The rest of the staff are upset . . .'

The British do not reveal their real emotions easily but it is necessary in this case. The message will only carry weight if the feeling is perceived as real and demanding of attention within the relationship.

We are within our rights to state our feelings if they are strong enough. However we are often not in touch with our feelings, maybe because it is British not to display them. It can help, if we have an intimate relationship with someone, if we try to discuss our honest feelings with them in order to identify them.

There is sometimes a belief that if we show our feelings we make ourselves vulnerable. The point about the assertive message is that we choose to reveal our feelings when we are within our rights. We should not use this technique if the other person does not regard us highly enough to feel inclined to take some action to keep or improve our mutual relationship. If there is no goodwill or the person we are trying to change does not care about our relationship, then almost any message, barring the use of force, is bound to fail.

# Behaviour

If somebody's behaviour is upsetting us and we want them to change it then we must describe that behaviour — we need to state the real issue that is the cause of the problem. This issue must be evidence that is not open to dispute, otherwise the power of the message is lost in an argument about the facts. We may often have to do some research before such an assertive message and this could involve talking with the person.

- **e.g.** You: 'My records show that you have been late six times this month.'

  Other: 'Yes, that's right, but never over half an hour!'

  You: 'Well, that may be so but I am very worried that . . .' etc.

There are some other rules on this essential component of an assertive (confrontative) message.

- It should be an accurate statement of facts, not opinions or values.

  **e.g.** 'When you started speaking before I had finished . . .'

*not*  'When you should have kept quiet . . .'

**e.g.** 'When you only finished three-quarters of the work that Fred did . . .'

*not*  'When you don't pull your weight . . .'

- It should be specific, not implied or veiled.

  **e.g.** 'When you tidied up my papers . . .'

  *not*  'When you hid my papers . . .'

  **e.g.** 'When you overspent your budget . . .'

  *not*  'When you fritter our money away over the budget . . .'

- It should be non-judgemental and as impersonal as possible.

  **e.g.** 'When you didn't call me to let me know you'd be late . . .'

  *not*  'When you ignore me by not telling me you'll be late . . .'

  *or*  'When you don't think it is necessary to call me to tell me you'll be late . . .'

- It must be exact, not absolute.

  **e.g.** 'When you were late three times last week . . .'

  *not*  'When you're always late . . .'

- It should be as brief as possible in order to retain the impact of the whole message. If you have a lot of evidence, just give a summary rather than chapter and verse of each incident.

  **e.g.** 'When our last five meetings have overrun by a minimum of half an hour each . . .'

  *not*  'When at the meeting five weeks ago, we overran by forty-two minutes and . . . etc.'

- It should be about the real issues with the right person; many people in Britain talk about symptoms rather than confronting a person with the real problem (non-assertive).

> **e.g.** 'When you did not respond to three questions I
>         directed at you and looked out of the window.'
> *not* 'When the meeting with me seemed a bit offhand.'

# Effects

The last essential part of the message is to give the person
we would like to change a good reason for changing. If the
effect is missed out, the message loses its power. The
reaction can be:

- 'So you feel upset when I do this – but that's life.'

We have to give people a convincing reason if we want
them to take action. The following guidelines apply to this
part of the message.

- It must be a tangible reason.
  **e.g.** 'Other people have started turning up late too.'
  *not* 'It is having a poor effect on morale.'
- Again it must be non-judgemental fact rather than
  opinion or value.

It has the same rules as for behaviour.

- **e.g.** 'And output has dropped by 12 per cent.'
  *not* 'We're losing most of our production.'
  **e.g.** 'Because I have to spend five minutes tidying up.'
  *not* 'Because I'm always having to clear up after you.'

# Personal reason

This is another optional part of the message (together with the 'best reason' for behaviour). It involves strengthening the reasoning behind the effects by adding the most telling effect on the receiver, if known. It is an appeal to their known needs.

- e.g.  Effect 'I am now two days behind with my work
         schedule . . .' Personal reason '. . . which includes that
         financial report that you wanted quickly.'

Some messages only have a very general effect in which case it is worth pointing out that there is a personal effect as this will provide greater incentive to change.

# Consequences

If we need to put a very strong reason into our message in order to change another person, we can consider stating the actions that will be taken if there is no change. The consequence has to be credible to the other person, as when the mother says to the child, 'It will be early to bed for you', and the child knows that this will happen if they don't provide a solution.

Managers can think of many consequences that they can use, such as:

- 'I will have to start formal disciplinary procedures.'
- 'I will withdraw my staff from the project.'

- 'I cannot recommend you for promotion.'
- 'I will not proceed with this matter.'

Because it is an honest statement rather than a threat, it is important to have neutral, factual, reasonable non-verbal communication, even though the words may seem aggressive. It will thus give the other person the chance of providing a solution before the consequence is realised.

## THE COMPLETE MESSAGE

We can now look at the message, with all the ingredients put together. It is not important in which order we have them as long as the essential ones of:

- the 'I' message
- feelings
- behaviour
- effects

are included. The wording is, as mentioned, a matter of personal judgement, dependent on the common under-standable language used with the other person.

Some examples of assertive messages designed to change behaviour in different situations are (the optional parts are in brackets):

- '(I am really pleased that you have got a hobby but) when you leave all the pieces in our living room it makes me very unhappy because that is the only room that we all share and can use for guests.'
- 'I (know you like to get back to your family straight after

work, but I) am very annoyed when you don't tidy your work space before you leave, because it makes more work for me (and I often have to leave some of my work over for you).'

- '(I know that you are very busy and have a lot of demands on your time but) I am very upset because, when you have to answer the phone during our daily meetings, it means that they take at least half an hour over our planned time and I am getting behind with my work (which includes the report you want).'

- '(I realise that you work as hard as, if not harder than, any of the other staff, but) I am upset because you have been at least twenty minutes late three times in the last fortnight and this has had a bad effect on the timekeeping of at least two of the other staff whom I have talked to (besides not being in accordance with your terms of employment).'

- '(I can appreciate that you are trying to put your argument as strongly as possible but) I am very worried because you have not responded to my proposals and arguments but have kept your demands the same. If this continues I will (reluctantly) see no further point in our discussing the matter.'

# THE SIX-STEP APPROACH

We have learned how to compose an assertive message to change someone's behaviour, but what happens if it is ignored or does not work in some other way? This is the question that most managers raise on assertiveness training courses.

Like many of our communication skills, the assertive message fits into a wider framework. In the same way as making a speech involves more than just knowing what to say, we have to look at other aspects. These can be considered in a chronological order.

1. Prepare beforehand.
2. Send the message.
3. Use silence.
4. Listen reflectively.
5. Recycle the process.
6. Focus on solutions.

# 1. Prepare beforehand

The first thing to consider before composing an assertive message to alter someone's behaviour is our relationship with the other person and the need for change.

- What is your relationship: the trust level: will you be trespassing?
- Do you need the message: is it a persistent concern: is it a trivial or major matter?

It probably is not worth bothering if the problem is with somebody who keeps interrupting you when you are speaking, if they are a stranger who does not affect your life and whom you will probably never see again.

If the decision is that there is a need for change within the relationship, then we should consider:

- The content of the message. Many people write short notes or key points because this helps them think calmly about the language and get it right. By using only key points

they don't lose too much spontaneity. In order not to
speak the written word, only the key words are written.
They might practise saying it aloud until they are happy
with the message and feel that they can give it to the
person they have in mind.

There is nothing artificial about thinking about what we
want to say, and even rehearsing parts that we know will
arise. I can remember doing just such a thing when I was
very small and wanted extra pocket money. I still do
prepare and practise in my mind before any important
interview or meeting.

The other thing I can remember doing as a child was
picking my time and place when asking for more money.
Was my father in a good mood? Was he (a dentist) with a
patient? If he was with, but not working on, a patient it
increased my chances as he would like to look generous and
kind to support his image as a dentist (appeal to self-
interest!). So we have to consider:

- making an appointment or ensuring that you have enough
  time to deal with any likely reaction to your message
- where you can be private
- home, neutral, or the other person's ground
- what mood they are in and time of day, relating to stress
  and amenability

## 2. Send the message

There is a British habit of making 'small talk' before
getting down to business. This is quite good practice to
relax someone, for example a stranger off their home

ground. However, in the case of an assertive confrontation message it would only serve to make the message more of a surprise or to 'catch them off their guard' if they were relaxed. As such it would be seen as devious manipulation. If the small talk is overdone it can even weaken the effect of the message by making it seem an afterthought that can be ignored. Similarly, if an appointment has been made, it is likely to be seen through, in which case small talk will serve no purpose at all.

Establishing wavelength by the use of small talk is thus not relevant here; we can do this within the message by giving the best reason for the person's behaviour if we think this is appropriate. If we want to be assertive, it is best to start directly with our message, after a suitable conversation opener to get the other person's attention.

- **e.g.** 'Hello . . . I wanted to talk to you about something that has been bothering me . . .'

The other vital ingredient in sending the message, as previously discussed, is the non-verbal communication. This may suit and give impact to our message. We need to consider our posture, positioning and surroundings, eye contact, expression, gestures and vocal content.

# 3. Use silence

Some British people feel very awkward about silences in face-to-face communication. They feel that they must talk to fill the embarrassing silence. However silence, properly used, can often be more powerful than words.

As discussed in the section on listening, passive listening

can become disconcerting to a speaker. It is entirely appropriate, though, after giving a confrontative message. It gives the other person time to think and, ideally, to come up with a solution that satisfies you both. If you were to talk there would be the problem of diluting the message and possibly of giving them a 'hook' to hang a defensive response on. The message is self-contained and has all the necessary ingredients; any additional elements will weaken the case and may well provide an 'escape route'.

The effect of silence (passive listening) is thus to indicate that we have delivered our honest, direct message about our problem and that we are awaiting an answer. It is the best way to make our point.

# 4. Listen reflectively

If we send an assertive message, hoping to change someone's behaviour, we are expecting a response which contains a mutually acceptable solution. This should not be a compromise, with both parties conceding, but collaboration (as with synergy) to get the best possible answer. However, with some people (who may feel happy or guilty about their behaviour) we may elicit a response that is not collaborative. This will happen especially where the other person's normal responses are defensive or aggressive towards anybody whom they perceive as challenging their 'status quo'. Most people at work know a few of these people; they are the ones who have a defensive excuse/reason for any action and who will almost automatically attack another's position as a reaction.

The main way to deal with these responses is to listen reflectively to them. This has the effect of not changing our position, while maintaining empathy and freeing the other person from an emotional reaction so that they can deal with our problem logically.

## Aggressive responses

It is important to reflect the feeling or hostile emotion, as well as the content, in such a response. This has the effect of showing that we have registered their stated feeling and gives them a chance to modify any exaggeration. It helps them to become reasonable.

- **e.g.**    Response to message: 'I happen to like what I do and think you have no right at all to talk to me like this.'

    You:    'You feel that I am wrong to tell you my problem because you are happy with what you do.'

Like the message, the reflective response must be non-judgemental to be effective in removing the emotion from the response. It should *not* be:

- **e.g. You:**    'You feel that it is none of my business if you behave inconsiderately.'

This will just fuel an argument.

The other person must be treated with respect (assertively) but must not be allowed to sidetrack us from our point. If the hostile response is an attempt to draw us on to weaker ground, then we may have to use one of the techniques for coping with critics, such as fogging or negative assertion, before returning to our point.

- **e.g.**     Response to message: 'You're one to talk! What about you last week at that important meeting?'
  - **You:**     'That may be so (fogging) but I still feel upset . . .'
  - **or You:**     'Well, I agree that I did make rather a mess of that meeting (negative assertion) but right now I want to talk about my problem. I still feel . . .'

These can be used when a reflective response such as 'You think that we should be discussing my behaviour at the meeting' might be seen as unconstructive in finding a solution.

## Defensive responses

By listening reflectively to defensive response we can achieve several things. For example, we can retain our empathy by showing that we have heard their response. This shows respect for the person, an essential ingredient of assertiveness.

- Response to message: 'Well, I don't see that my coming in late causes such a big problem in the office.'
  - **You:** 'You feel that your timekeeping doesn't have an effect on the other staff.'

A response of this type is better than the instant put down of saying:

- **e.g. You:**     'Well, I do!' (This is an aggressive response which may be appropriate in other circumstances.)

If our reflective response draws no answer then we may well have to use our skill in saving face before restating our case (on factual evidence).

- **e.g. You:** 'Well I can understand that it may seem to you that your timekeeping doesn't have an effect but I have checked over the last two weeks and . . .'

The reflective response also can often draw out more facts. These can sometimes make reassertion unnecessary.

- **e.g.** Response to message: 'I think it was only seven times that it happened and anyway the last time was because I had been driving all night and hadn't got time to prepare?'
  
  **You:** 'So one of the seven times was caused because you hadn't prepared?'

This exchange seems to be heading towards getting a solution generated by the receiver of the message.

Again, it is important not to be sidetracked by questions or issues which are not directly relevant to the problem. We have to use the skills such as fogging and negative assertion, together with broken record.

- **e.g.** Defensive response: 'Well, what about all the others who come in late . . . you haven't talked to them yet.'
  
  **You:** 'Well, that may be so, but . . .'
  
  **or You:** 'Yes, I should have talked to them first and I *will* talk to them after, but . . .'

If the defensive response takes the form of withdrawal, the same techniques apply, but in this case all we can reflect is the non-verbal communication and silence before re-asserting our message.

- **e.g.**    Defensive response of silence.
  **You:**    (After also responding with silence for a long period) 'You feel that you can't give me an answer but I've still got the problem . . .'

The technique of reflective listening to defensive or aggressive responses has the effect of helping us find out more about our relationship and thus makes it easier to find mutual ground.

# 5. Recycle the process

The technique of broken record is used to re-assert our message until we get a satisfactory response. Persistence in standing up for our rights is part of assertiveness; we keep returning to our message until we generate a solution. This may take, in some cases, up to ten repetitions. It is always possible to allow some time to lapse between repetitions, but if the time is too long it will detract from the urgency of our message.

- In a recent experiment when someone was deliberately playing loud music late in the evening in a student block, most students didn't complain. Of those that did, most gave up when their needs weren't met after the first complaint. A very few complained twice, and it was only the one or two who had the persistence to complain a third time that got their needs met by the music being turned down.

There is a rhythm to recycling a message to try to change someone's behaviour.

- Send the message.
- Silence.
- Listen reflectively to defensive or aggressive responses.
- Re-send the message.
- Silence.
- Listen reflectively to responses which are not solutions,
  and so on until solutions are offered.

The listening stage should not be overdone because this may be interpreted as accommodating behaviour. Again, if the repetition of the message is made after minimal listening it may be interpreted as aggressive.

At the very worst we will have made our feelings and concern very evident. Even if no satisfactory solution is offered, our position will be well understood within the relationship. We will have honestly stated our rights over something that was serious and persistent enough to damage our relationship.

If there is any goodwill present in the relationship then a solution will be offered. As the solution is not imposed, there is more chance of it being adhered to if accepted.

## 6. Focus on solutions

The sender should concentrate on any solution that is offered by the receiver. Although we should persist until we get a solution that is satisfactory to us, we do not want to appear unreasonable or over-insistent. The technique is first to reflect back any solution offered, in order to check the sender's understanding. Secondly we check it with our needs (problem) to assess whether they will be met.

- **e.g.**     Response to message: 'Well, I will make up my lateness by working late.'
  - **You:**     'So you are offering to stay later to work the time you are late coming?'
  - **Response:**     'Yes.'
  - **You:**     'I can see that would make up the work content, but what I am upset about is that your coming in late has started to affect the other staff. Some of them have been coming in late now and we need to have the office fully staffed at 8.30 a.m.'

We are looking for the best solution, although of course there may have to be bargaining in order to achieve a workable compromise (mentioned at the end of Chapter 2) if this ideal cannot be achieved.

If a mutually acceptable solution is arrived at, it is not necessary for the atmosphere to be pleasant and cheerful as much as sincere. Of course, it is normal courtesy to thank the recipient of the message for the solution, after we have reflected it to check the understanding. Furthermore, it is often useful to establish a review period for the agreed action, especially when we are using these techniques at work. Most managers would confirm the agreed solution and review period in writing.

The best assertive solution is one that is offered by the person we are trying to change. Of course, we may achieve our solution more quickly by aggression (using power) but only by invading other people's rights. Assertiveness is not the imposition of our solution on another, which only requires a yes or no answer; it is a technique which is aimed at getting a positive suggestion of action from another. If we persist within our rights, then we can achieve a solution which will be part of better communication and understanding between ourselves and others. This in turn will lead to better relationships based on trust. This must be a key skill for any manager who has to achieve results through other people.

# 13

# LEARNING AND USING ASSERTIVENESS SKILLS

When we are small children, most of us have a protective family which gives us a perfect atmosphere in which to experiment and learn. Our attempts are encouraged and our mistakes are not thrown back at us in a serious way. Subsequently, at school we again have an environment which includes teaching, experimentation and learning in behaviour. Through both these periods we are programmed, conditioned and learn all sorts of behaviour and responses which are going to influence our relationships and success in life. It is well documented that many adults who do not have great social skills and relationships often had a childhood where some element of a good learning atmosphere was not present.

Most of us develop the majority of our behaviour traits and responses by the time we are young adults. It then becomes increasingly difficult for most of us to learn and adopt new skills. This is also made more difficult because, once we have left our early protective environment and entered the 'cruel hard world', failure is not tolerated as before. Failure is regarded as part of the learning process for children – parents erupting into joy at their baby's mispronunciations, for example. This enables children to learn without the bad feelings associated with failure.

As we get older the consequences of failure are taken more seriously. This is probably because we make decisions of more consequence. We get more critical of each other and it becomes harder to admit failure, to the extent that people deny it even when the rest of the world is aware of it. This happens especially with public figures such as politicians and management and union leaders. Of course, assertiveness gives you the techniques of fogging, negative assertion and negative enquiry to cope with criticism, possible and sometimes real failure while not losing your self-esteem, but these are not common skills.

Perhaps it is this terrible fear of failure that makes so many people nervous about public speaking. It is certainly a big factor in preventing people from learning new social and behaviour skills as adults.

If you have felt that most of this book is not for you and you don't need these sort of skills in your life, I wonder what the underlying reasons are? Listen for the defensive or aggressive responses in your answers — even to the words and thoughts you have in your head.

- I'm too long in the tooth to change!
- I don't really (listen to the vocals) have problems with my relationships.
- Most of this is a lot of mumbo-jumbo!
- I don't really have the time.
- Yes — but will it work in my situation?
- I can't see that changing things for me.
- All very well in theory . . .
- People have to take me as I am.

This list is endless.

Certainly, only you can change yourself. If you, whatever your age, would (or think you would) like to become proficient in the skills in this book, I have listed some tips.

# THE NEED

As already stated, most of us, however deficient we may think ourselves, have a high level of skills. We can register disapproval of people's advances, both physical and psychological, in a variety of ways. Some of these may be instinctive and some learned.

What we have to look for are the areas where we would like to improve our performance in relationships, whether social or at work. Many relationships may be good or satisfactory, but can you recognise those where you don't achieve satisfaction, or in which you would like to be more open and honest? Do you have a particular situation where you cannot speak your mind, although you feel you would be right to do so? Do you feel that the only method of obtaining your way and succeeding in life is by manipulating and dominating people? These are some of the signals that another (assertive) approach is needed.

Assertiveness and the ability to influence people are not going to solve all your problems or make all your relationships successful. These skills are concerned with being happier with yourself and in your relationships in life. They are also concerned with treating people as they want to be treated and, by the same mark, respecting yourself as you do others.

It does not involve a constant attempt to be 'assertive' in all you say and do; rather it involves a choice of behaviour options to suit situations. We already do this in many ways. The parents, deciding how to treat their child who has offended again have to decide whether to: treat it as an adult; scold it like a child; give up; ignore the offence; punish the child; try and reform by dominating. All parents have faced this problem.

The options and techniques detailed in this book can be the better answer to the occasional, and in some people's lives recurring, problems. Indeed the only person I ever met who had evolved an almost constant assertive personality had a job in charge of 'children in care'. She was able to compose assertive messages to change behaviour quite naturally. It was her normal response. When I asked her how she had learned this skill, she said that she must have developed it by trial and error. She had never analysed it as we have in this book, but, as she said, 'It works, doesn't it!' In fact, she claimed that it was the only technique that did work with her charges.

There is certainly more concern these days with outward looks. There are multimillion-pound businesses in cosmetics and diet and figure control; many people spend hours making themselves up and dressing externally, getting themselves in shape, often by methods that seem like torture, solely so that they can portray the exact image that they want to project. However, very few of these people judge others by anything else but their behaviour — what they say and do. The British all belong to social classes and working groups which to some extent dictate their behaviour, dress, houses and standards, but when we judge each other as people within these classifications, it is according to our social and communication skills. We give people respect and, therefore authority according to how they handle people and situations.

Assertiveness, rather than aggressive or accommodating behaviour, is not common in Britain and can be an invaluable asset in gaining the respect of others; it can be far more valuable than any amount of external change. Self-esteem is also a vital component of physical and mental health.

Most people are content with their ability to deal successfully with the majority of people and situations. It is the difficult ones that matter! It is when they really want to be able to make their point, when it is important to them to deal with a difficult person or situation, that they may need assertiveness, in the same way as do the bus conductors on trouble routes or many managers at work.

The first thing is to decide your own need to learn any of the skills that may be new to you. Without a perceived need, this book is academic. Assertion and influencing skills are certainly not that; they are practical measures.

YOU HAVE TO DECIDE THERE IS A NEED

# CONFIDENCE AND DETERMINATION

Anyone who has trained a child in some skill will know that confidence and determination are vital to success. The child who says 'I can't do it' when learning to swim or ride a bicycle is the one who is going to be the most difficult to train, as it is very much a self-fulfilling prophecy. World class athletes not only have talent but also confidence and determination in great quantities. During the Sarajevo Winter Olympics (1984) I noticed the comments of three winners.

• The East German Stetti Martin, who won the Women's Single Luge gold medal, said 'It was my ability to concentrate that won me the title.' The event, however, was a run of less than three-quarters of a minute on each of four days.

- The Canadian speed skater, Gaeten Brucher, after winning his second gold medal of the games, the Men's 1500 metres, said, 'My legs began to go stiff and I did the last lap on guts and determination.'
- The winner of the Men's Downhill Skiing, the American Bill Johnson, previously regarded as an underdog in the contest, said after he had finished, 'I've been talking big all week and now I've finally done it.'

We all know that if we feel we can do something and are determined to do our best, we have a far greater chance of achieving it. I recently heard a much travelled writer on the radio talking about his adventures and some of the moments in which he had been in danger. The interviewer asked him how he had got out of a particularly difficult situation when he was being interrogated by drunken soldiers for three hours in a troubled African city. He said he found that 'if you act with a certain amount of confidence and give a certain amount of respect' you could resolve most difficult situations.

It is necessary therefore not only to appreciate the need for developing your assertiveness and influencing skills but also to *be confident and determined that you can*.

## PRACTICE AND EASY STAGES

Overconfidence, however, can be equally as much of a handicap. The British tend to dislike people whom they consider braggarts. In the early days of that great boxer

Cassius Clay (later named Muhammad Ali) there were many who only watched him in the hope that he might be beaten. His statement 'I'm the Greatest' brought great numbers of fans to watch him box Henry Cooper. Although Cooper was beaten in the end, they will long remember his putting Clay on his back. However Clay (as Ali) later became very popular in Britain when he lived up to the majority of his boasts.

Most of us develop our skills in the same way as we learn to play a musical instrument, by stages. Of course, there are always people with exceptional talent who can acquire skills without much effort, but for most of us we have to practise very hard.

I was watching my colleague, Sandy, helping her child Alexandra to walk the other day. Minutes later I was running down the stairs at her house. We reflected that at one stage all our skills such as walking and running down stairs were very difficult and had to be learned, often with quite painful mistakes. Sandy was not teaching Alexandra to run down stairs first but, instinctively, taking the learning process in stages. Sandy and I, on the other hand, could take it for granted that if we programmed our mind to 'go across the room' or 'run down the stairs' we did not have to do anything else to achieve it but let our minds follow our automatic physical response to our brain's wish. We did not analyse the detail of our physical movements, and might well have fallen down the stairs if we had. In contrast, Alexandra had to concentrate on each step of walking. She had to have the need, which was provided by Sandy moving a little way away and encouraging her, as well as concentration and determination, to complete her few steps upright to Sandy.

For many of us there is a parallel experience, as adults,

in learning to drive a car. The many individual actions that we have to take before starting a car and moving off are terribly difficult for most of us to learn at first. Frequently an essential can be overlooked. Once we have passed our test, though, and gained valuable driving practice, we find that we can drive while talking to another person or listening to a programme on the radio. We have absorbed the detailed actions which we consciously repeated so many times and, by just willing the result of the action, our subconscious mind will follow the required programme.

The same principles apply to learning life skills. Some of these may be inherent, as with some non-verbal communication or easily acquired. For the majority of us, learning most life skills, including assertion and influencing skills, requires the same conscious effort as learning to drive before we can use them subconsciously.

A high level of assertiveness and of ability to influence others is rare in Britain, perhaps because very few people develop them in early life and later on it seems too hard. Such people have the capability of easily adopting an accommodating or aggressive posture, and even when this does not quite fit the bill within relationships at work, or in social life, they are reluctant to attempt another behaviour. Perhaps this is because there is no longer the safe and controlled environment found when learning to walk or learning to drive. There is greater fear of failure and its consequences.

The solution is to start learning new skills in easy stages, in safe situations. This is the value of training courses; a good training course, rather than being critical of course members, is intent on guiding them and letting them practise so that they can feel confident with their new skills.

The environment is controlled and support and guidance are provided by the tutor.

If you are going to learn the skills in this book without such guidance and help, then you have to choose your time and situation. In the same way as you don't choose the busiest road in which to start learning to drive, it is much easier to start by trying such skills out within a relationship that is very secure and in low-risk situations. Eventually you will be able to gain confidence and it will become, like walking, a very natural thing. You will be able to programme your mind with your wish to adopt a particular behaviour or response in order to create the impression you want, and your subconscious will respond.

This is not to say that there is no conscious effort involved. As with most communication skills, such as being polite or deferential to someone, you have to use your conscious mind but it comes to you much more easily with practice. Eventually these skills become part of you; your second nature.

To start using assertiveness and influencing skills we need to:

- choose a safe relationship and situation
- practise
- develop the skills in easy stages

until we gain a natural expertise.

# 14

# SOME USEFUL CONCEPTS

## THE EFFECTS OF EMOTIONS ON OUR REASONING – OR SEEING RED

One of the marvellous skills that most humans learn is the ability to communicate concepts and ideas to each other. This is what I am trying to do with symbols (English words) in this book. Many studies have shown that, whereas this method is sufficient for some, others will find it more helpful and memorable to have a visual representation. One of the basic premises of memory courses, learning theory (especially those well-advertised, short-term language courses) and neuro-linguistic programming (NLP) books is that we all develop preferred learning styles (see book list *Introducing NLP*) – a mixture of seeing, hearing, doing and feeling. This is the basis of the fact that all memory systems are based on connecting left-hand side (LHS) brain cortex (outer surface of the brain) to right-hand side (RHS) brain cortex.

We now have machines which can chart brain activity. When a baby is born, it has overall cortex activity which starts to locate itself according to what the baby is doing.

When the baby starts to hear words, an artificial system

in which sounds change according to which language is used, the activity locates in the LHS. This is because all the functions that computers can do are mainly located in the LHS brain. The RHS brain has mainly different functions. Diagrammatically this can be represented, with some of the activities, as in Figure 14.1.

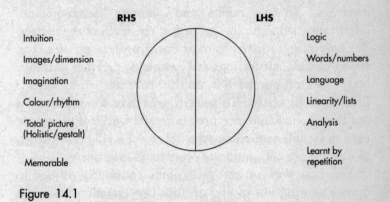

Figure 14.1

Some of the functions are depicted above (they may be a bit mixed with left-handed people) and all are not completely exclusive to a brain's hemisphere. Research indicates that the RHS brain 'total' pictures include feelings, intuition and emotion.

A great simplification would be to say that the RHS is concerned with Feelings and the LHS with Facts.

The relevance to assertiveness is that the brain functions electrochemically. Different feelings generate different chemicals which affect our brain functions. Our body clock generates different hormones which affect our brain performance. This makes us prefer some activities to others at different times of the day. In the same way, different feelings generate different chemicals, with different effects on the brain.

If you get angry, depressed or stressed, it is difficult, if not impossible, to behave normally and logically. In the same way, if someone else is angry or emotional with you, it is usually impossible for you to talk logically with them until the emotion has subsided.

The RHS brain is very useful for memory, but is the reason why logic often gets forgotten in our discussions and meetings. Scoring points and winning become more important than logic and getting at the truth of the matter. We only have to listen to most Parliamentary debates. The effects of different feelings and emotions, together with our body clock on our RHS brain, can enhance or impede our LHS brain functions. To access the LHS reasoning brain of our friends, acquaintances, relations and work colleagues we need to be able to dissipate the unhelpful RHS brain effects, so that we can communicate openly and assertively.

The best way to get your point considered is not to oppose an idea, but to find genuine (honest) merit in it and then propose your option (see page 8). This is the principle basic to methods of argument (see page 25).

## THAT'S THE LIMIT

Another concept which has helped me to understand assertiveness within different cultures is to depict 'psychological space' (see page 10) pictorially. It can help you to understand why some behaviour is acceptable from some people, but perceived as aggressive from others and how our permitted personal boundaries vary with different relationships. Why some seemingly aggressive words can be exchanged within a relationship without offence or damage. Indeed, this seemingly scoring-points behaviour can be the very basis of a relationship. Do you not know friends and partners who exchange digs and criticisms regularly within their relationships. How about you?

If you take the four categories of physical, territorial space (see page 7), you can represent them for psychological space diagrammatically to show how close you allow people to the real you (see Figure 14.2)

The furthest category is for those people with whom you do not want a relationship, people whom you would rather avoid or dislike. Our language reflects our desire for this distance depending on the strength of our dislike:

- 'I try to steer clear of him/her.'
- 'I give him/her a wide berth.'
- 'Clear off!'

As it does with our relationships:

- 'We drifted apart.'
- 'He/she was very distant.'
- 'We were/became very close.'

The next category moving nearer to your real self is 'public'. This, like all categories, has a number of subdivisions. The public category ranges from strangers with whom you have no antipathy, apart from your reserve, to people whom you work with. The crucial criterion is the language that you use. Starting from formal, for the furthest people, it can be quite warm and friendly, but always ritual:

- People to whom you give a greeting out of politeness.
- People with whom you exchange a few words, often ritually about the weather in Britain.

- People whom we meet occasionally and always have a few
  words, which can sometimes be even jokingly mildly rude
  or offensive.
- Work colleagues whom you meet regularly, or even work
  with every day: you only talk with them about work or
  business matters. In these relationships a greeting such as,
  'How are you?' is delivered ritually and gets the ritual
  response such as, 'Fine' or 'Pretty good', no matter what is
  happening in your life. On a holiday I met an ex-primary
  school teacher who used to greet our table in the morning
  with a ritually enthusiastic 'Good morning. How are we?
  All well I trust'. I was tempted to say something
  outrageous, but resisted, knowing that it would only get a
  'nurturing parent' response (see book list *I'm OK, You're
  OK*).

In fact, holidays are a wonderful occasion to see and hear
these relationships establish and sometimes change.

The difference between public and the next section
'social' is that you seek the company or society of people in
the social category. It is, of course, closer to you. This
category includes most of the people whom we list as our
friends. Certainly I notice the difference because I always
include a few extra words in my Christmas cards. I send
them birthday cards. These people range from work colleagues whom you lunch with, by choice, to people you
know very well and are at times the friends that you see
most of. You talk with them about social matters as well as
about work and with those that are closer to you, about
even more private matters.

The difference between social relationships and the next
category 'personal' can be best defined by considering how

much the relationship depends on you being in the society of the other person. This is usually easier to assess in retrospect when it has been tested. Personal relationships will usually not be affected by distance or time. Within a short time, common ground based on mutual experiences is re-established, and you are communicating on the same wavelength as before. Social relationships fade if one of you puts distance and time between you. If you have been friendly with someone at one time and have lost touch because one of you moved, then this was a relationship in the social category.

- We can meet people and be very friendly on holidays, exchanging addresses when we part. This does not necessarily mean that we wish to continue as close a relationship when we return home. Indeed, we may be surprised if they turned up on our doorstep to stay for a time, only anticipating exchanging cards. We would probably welcome them on the original basis on another holiday. The social relationship is affected by place and time.

Personal relationships are with your very close friends. With them you can share many personal secrets and feelings and these relationships usually last for a long time, even through separations. For most of us there are very few in this category.

There are even fewer in the next section, which is 'intimate'. In this category, we have such a close relationship that we mutually have no secrets from each other; we are completely honest and open.

Common ground is the basis for establishing all

relationships and determining which category a particular one is in. No relationship is permanent because we and others change with age.

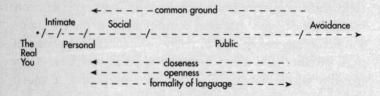

Figure 14.2

We can imagine ourselves like onions, with many skins around our centre: the inner you. With each person we decide how close we would like them to be and how much of ourselves we wish to reveal. The formality of our speech, (as well as the tone, etc.) changes with our relationships. Just think how you speak to strangers, asking directions, a business meeting, a business friend, a good friend, a loved person and a member of your family. If you can pretend they are there and speak out aloud as you would normally, you should find that you change your voice and words according to your relationships. As in the examples in Chapter 1 (see pages 11–13), we use different forms of address to indicate this space.

- Two young women decided to continue their tour of Africa
  after they had been abandoned by their partners at the
  start of their trek. They reported that when they arrived at
  settlements, they could tell how they were going to be
  treated by listening to the tone of the Africans, without
  knowing the languages. This helped them succeed by
  choosing and using the correct behaviour assertively.

- Imagine parents with a young girl called Jennifer, or diminutive Jenny, or pet name Twinkle. They are in the country and the daughter asks if she can explore a bit. The parents say, 'OK, but don't go too far away — we're going to leave in five minutes.' Five minutes go by and they give her a call. Firstly 'Twinkle, Twinkle, time to leave': you can imagine the caring tone of voice. Secondly, more worriedly 'Jenny, Jenny, we're going.' Then, 'Jennifer, come here at once,' strongly and impatiently. Finally 'Now look here Miss . . .' We should all be able to identify with this.

- Do you have somebody close to you, who uses a more formal name with you to express disapproval, or anger? If you do, the very use of it, combined with the tone of voice should tell you that you are 'in trouble'. They are expressing their criticism of your behaviour by temporarily distancing your relationship. This can be very effective in close relationships.

Allowing people closer to us and being more open with them has its risks. It is easier for them to hurt us. It is relatively easier to cope with verbal aggression from a comparative stranger than somebody close to you, whom you value and respect. You are more vulnerable. People who are very close, who hurt people deeply in relationships, can cause what I call scar tissue on their imaginary 'onion' layers. With a bad experience, many people will say 'never again' and be very wary and reluctant to allow a similar relationship to get as close to them.

Allowing a very close relationship to develop, because you are more open and vulnerable, requires far more mutual trust. It depends on mutual respect. This is the essence of assertiveness; respect for yourself and others; respect in action and words and thereby developing trust. If you think about people that you have problems with, then I am sure that, if you analyse their behaviour, you will agree that it has a basis in lack of respect and therefore of trust.

The closer people are to you, the more you require their respect and trust and they yours. Our mutual behaviour in successful relationships needs to be permitted and accepted.

This is an important concept in assertiveness; for each relationship we have our Permitted Limit. These vary with each relationship and can be often under review and negotiation. Just think how many times a day people want to change somebody else's behaviour or try to do it. When did you last criticise someone's behaviour towards you, or say what behaviour you would prefer. The vital thing is that you have a Preferred Permitted Limit for every person that you know.

- If you think about some of your friends and acquaintances, you could put them quite accurately into the categories in Figure 14.2 and also place them within the sections.

Of course relationships change with experience, distance, time and age:

- When I was very young, my mother was in my intimate section; I shared all my secrets, problems and hopes with her. About the age of six to eight this began to change. I would devise plans, sometimes with friends, so that Mum didn't know. In my early teens it was Gerry, at school, who knew all about my feelings, thoughts and crushes. I wonder where he is now.
- Children, when they start developing their own reasoning ability, often try to move their permitted limit for a

that they find it very difficult to say no and stand up for their rights. They treat themselves in a way that they would not ask of others. They often get 'lumbered' by others who take them for granted. But, even worse, they will take on difficult or tedious work themselves because they are afraid of the reaction of others if they ask them to do it, or for help. They end up resentfully submissive, ready to complain to whoever will listen, but not to change their behaviour.

- You may well have had a teacher, who could not keep order. He or she may make mild appeals to the class, but aggressive and manipulative pupils know when this can be ignored. The teacher loses the personal respect of the class, the very thing that they crave.

The lack of respect of others, coupled with self-blame for the perceived lack of success leads to a diminution of self-respect, thereby increasing the problem of passive behaviour (see book list *I'm OK, You're OK*). Quite often the person may resort to aggression in the form of an outburst to protest against the unfairness of the situation. This is not always to the person who is the cause of the submissive behaviour. The worsened relationships resulting can lead to a further loss of self-esteem.

**Avoidance** is when, as a result of having your limits exceeded, you try to avoid all situations where this may arise. Where aggression is unavoidable, people using avoidance behaviour stay quiet, knowing that there is nothing that they can do about it. They feel resentment, but their lack of self-respect means that they will take no action. Manipulative people take advantage of people who use avoidance behaviour in the same way as for submissive people. They will take their acquiescence for granted.

# ASSERTIVE BEHAVIOUR

**Assertive** behaviour is when you state your views, feelings and limits, while at the same time appreciating those of others. Respect is the key word. Self-respect to establish your limits with others, as well as respecting their limits. It is not about winning, but about trying honestly to reach mutual solutions through collaboration in which each other's concerns are considered.

This is why assertiveness is not effective if one party has no good will towards the other. This means that they have no respect for the other's wishes, limits and feelings. Hard negotiation or counter-aggression may be the way to earn respect. The problem for the normally passive person is that they have lost the respect of aggressive and manipulative people and to start adopting assertive behaviour is often perceived as counter-aggression. This can be difficult to start with for very passive people, but is a necessary step towards gaining respect (see book list *When I Say No, I Feel Guilty*).

Very passive people find it difficult to try out and adopt assertive behaviour as an option, because of their lack of self-respect. They are too conscious of their own weaknesses and supposed faults and of the rights, feelings and wishes of others.

If you don't have self-respect, how can you expect others to respect you? In other words, to be able to expect people to respect your limits you need to be able to respect them yourself. This means being able to state your limits reasonably and assertively. It is not a matter of winning or getting your own way, but stating your wishes reasonably. Rather than manipulation, it is an honest search for collaboration, in which your limits are an important factor to be considered.

It is very easy for those who have assertive skills to make what they think are helpful, constructive suggestions. However, this is only likely to increase the frustration of the person who uses mainly passive behaviour, even to the point where they have an aggressive argument. To help understand and overcome these difficulties I have found it useful to consider another concept diagrammatically.

# WE ARE NOT TOO OLD TO LEARN: ADDING TO OUR SKILLS

For the third concept I will adapt a representation of the learning process, which I have found in many books, in four stages and then relate each stage to assertiveness. The process is then diagrammatically represented in Figure 14.3.

## 1. Unconscious inability

When we are born, we have no idea of what we can or cannot do. It is difficult to tell what skills and talents we may have and develop. We cannot speak or drive, but at this stage, we are not conscious of our lack.

In adult life, we may wonder what skills and potential we may have and which we can still develop. There are many examples of people who have developed enormous talents later in life.

- Gauguin, the renowned painter, was a middle-class stock-broker, who abandoned his wife and career in his late thirties to pursue his art.

The relevance to assertiveness is to be aware that you could handle some parts of your life a bit better by learning the skills that other people use successfully. Assertiveness is not practised widely enough in Britain, a fact that I was made aware of when I got a job as a 'bouncer', to help pay for a year's course I was doing. First of all I was in awe of those who used the threat of aggression, or aggression, to get their wishes obeyed. Then I realised that some of my colleagues were getting the same results without even the threat.

## 2. Conscious inability

In order to start the process of learning we need two factors, Awareness and Need. There are many people who say that they cannot remember names, but remember faces, or vice versa. The skill of remembering both can be learned, as I have done (see book list *Make the Most of Your Mind*). They are aware of what they cannot do, however, and do not feel the need to change.

- Do you still make New Year resolutions? Many people break them and even give up making them. They are aware that they could improve, but do not have enough need and determination to succeed in every case.
- I have met many smokers who have told me that they have tried to give up, but failed. Their desire or need to give up was outweighed by their desire or need to smoke.

- Young children start associating various sounds (speech), that people in their lives make, with objects. When they realise that this helps them communicate better than their early noises, they learn to speak. They need to make their wants known.
- Most of us have learned to use sarcasm at an early age. We may not remember the process, but, we soon acquire a complex skill where, by intonation and expression, we can change the meaning of our words to the opposite of their literal meaning. We can say 'Thanks a lot' in many ways. We must have seen and heard someone use sarcasm and thought: I need to be able to do that.
- Many people, who have spent many long hours waiting for trains and buses, feel the need to learn to drive.

The relevance of this stage to assertiveness is to realise that we can learn different behaviours, which can give us more success and self-respect in life. This is what I learnt when I was a 'bouncer'. If you think that you have very few problems in relationships in your life, you may not practise assertive techniques of communication because you perceive no need. As a general comment, I feel it is better to have more options when faced with the varied situations that we can meet in life. However, learning depends on awareness and most of all need.

- When this book was first published, it was reviewed by someone very aggressively. It started with a complete falsehood stating that 'the author uses "assertiveness" in the same way as Americans use "aggression"'. It went on to condemn the book, first because of my varied career, then for the layout, but giving no comment on the content. It ended with the quotation: 'Most of this is a lot of mumbo-jumbo'. Clearly I did not inspire awareness or need in this reader. However, from the content of the review, I would be in favour of the person learning some assertive skills and using more logic, especially as it was published in *Work Study* magazine.

- On a course, there was a man who said he was 'too old to change his ways'. He also said that 'you can't teach an old dog new tricks'. This was a pity, for two reasons. First many others on the course said that they found him very difficult and unpleasant to work with; and second, because he thought that there was an age when you stopped learning.

## 3. Conscious ability

The next step in our learning process is to practise the skills and abilities that we want to learn. This can pose difficulties if we use the 'deep end' approach and try to use techniques immediately, without practise. Whereas this can be effective when the person already has many skills which they can adapt to the tasks, it can be disastrous if the person is *not* sufficiently skilled. The best learning needs, again, two vital elements. These are safety and fun.

- The best way to teach a baby to walk and talk is not to apply sanctions to him or her but to encourage and make the learning fun. We do not criticise the baby who mispronounces a word, or falls down after two wobbly steps. To help them progress, we enthuse, smile and urge them to persevere.
- Young children can be found practising words and phrases to themselves, before trying them out on friends and even

parents, until they get enough confidence to try it out for real.

- Learning to drive is often not a good learning experience with members of your family. The relationship can make it neither safe or fun. Most people go to a reputable driving school, who take you to quiet roads to try to ensure the safe element.

- If you think about your time at school, did you look forward to some classes? They were almost certainly the ones you did your best at. Was it the teacher, or the subject; and think about the skills that the teacher used. If they were really good, then you should be able to say that you achieved your success yourself.

At this stage of learning, when you use skills consciously there can be two drawbacks. Firstly, if you are thinking about the techniques that you are trying to use, it means part of your mind can be distracted from what you are really doing. Secondly, if you try consciously to explain to someone else a skill that you normally do without thinking, you can make mistakes, because you are no longer on 'automatic pilot'.

The relevance to assertiveness is, I hope, obvious. If you want to add assertiveness to your skills, then you need to be able to learn them in a safe environment. Going on a training course is one option. This can give you a reminder of the techniques involved and a chance to practise them without censure, or the consequences of real life. If you want to try them out in real life (not everybody likes role play), then it is best to follow the learning-to-drive example and try out the techniques in relatively safe situations.

The difficulties with this stage are that, as with learning to drive, you have to concentrate actively on what you are doing. In the same way that you use your rear-view mirror, you have originally to concentrate on the technique as much as the purpose. Also, if you think about what you do naturally, you may not be able to perform with your natural fluency and ease. If you have tried teaching somebody a skill that you take for granted, you will know what I mean. This is because of the last stage of the learning process.

## 4. Subconscious competence

Once again, there are two main elements in achieving the last stage of skill ownership. These are practice, which leads to confidence.

- When we learn and practise communication skills, such as sarcasm, we don't have to consider consciously, after a while, how we will manage the effect; it is completely inherent.
- It is possible to drive, especially on a route we know well, while listening to music, the radio, having a conversation, or thinking. We are driving on a sort of subconscious automatic pilot.
- Do you consciously concentrate on how you do up your shoelaces? Can you explain how to do it to someone else, without thinking first how you do this automatic skill?

It is the same with assertiveness. I have practised some skills until now I am completely happy with them. They are part of my natural choice of responses. I still feel a bit awkward about using the 'assertive message' to try to change people's behaviour (see Chapter 12), but on the eleven times that I have used it seriously, it has so far been successful. The message from the concept of the learning process is to start off using the skills of assertiveness in low-risk situations until you build up the confidence to tackle the problems that really bother you.

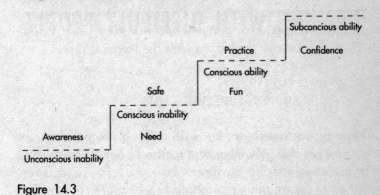

Figure 14.3

# 15

# DEALING WITH DIFFICULT PEOPLE

Some approaches to dealing with difficult people take some stereotypes and give advice on tactics to handle them. This is useful in that it illustrates how you can use different tactics to communicate successfully with different people. I find this helpful, but limiting.

I know some people like the stereotypes, but not exactly. Also, like you and me, they can change tactics. They may have a preferred type of behaviour, but if confronted, may change. They can try different tactics, just as we can. We have to consider what we can say and do, to try to get the result you want.

This is an important factor in assertiveness, if you are confronting somebody: it is important to think about the result that you would like. Also, results that you would settle for; this gives you some flexibility and room to arrive at a workable compromise (see page 34). If your normal reaction is to want to avoid the confrontation, or not to give offence, think about what you would like to happen. Visualising success can give you a better chance of achieving it (see book list *Introducing NLP*).

The next issue is to think about how you are going to behave and communicate in order to achieve this. If what you have done, or not done, to date has not worked to your satisfaction with someone, then change tactics.

Neuro-Linguistic Programming (NLP), which explores how we think and communicate, states that firstly, you should think about the result that you want in a situation (outcome). Secondly, you should be aware of all the reactions that you are receiving (acuity), and thirdly, you need to be flexible enough to keep changing your behaviour until you get the response that you want (flexibility). To adapt the author's words: If you always do the same thing with a person, you'll always get the same results. If this isn't to your liking, change what you do. Try some new communication.

We have a range of behaviours, which can be broadly classified into Aggressive, Passive and Assertive. We have the first two mostly programmed into us from an early age, and some people have developed the third. It is a reasoning skill, which is why many trainers and authors use 'Transactional analysis' (see book list *I'm OK, You're OK* and *Games People Play*). We are never too old to start adding more skills to our repertoire. The person who is going to succeed more in life is the person who has more responses to deal with different situations.

Most of the people I have met say that in the greatest part of their home, work and recreational life, they have no problems with their own or others' behaviour. This is how life should be. If the world was filled with accommodating people, then there would be nobody giving offence, we would all get on wonderfully. However, we would not be able to get through doors with other people because we would all be stuck; saying 'After you', 'No, please, after you'.

The world we know, though, has seemingly increased

numbers of people who are aggressive or manipulative (see Preface 2). Many organisations state that they have an aggressive marketing or other policy, and this might be a pointer as to what behaviour is encouraged. Competitiveness is a well-used word in the 1990s.

Many of us know people, whom we regularly work with, whose behaviour towards us we would like to change. We may come into contact, during our working day, with customers who are increasingly demanding and aggressive and find ourselves losing control. Or, we may reflect that, when dealing with friends, we occasionally would like to have handled our communication better; we would have preferred a different outcome.

It is a problem when your behaviour is a predictable, usual reaction to a recurring situation. An example is finding it difficult to say no. It is then that assertive techniques are invaluable and changing your behaviour gives you a great chance of being able to change the outcome and your relationships. These techniques enable you to put your case reasonably, while stating your preferred limits and respecting those of others. This gives you the best chance of earning the respect of others for your limits, thereby increasing your self-respect.

Although we may not need to adopt assertive behaviour for most of our lives, to be able to use the techniques competently we need to have practised and developed them until we have skill-ownership (see page 174 and 'We are not too old to learn' page 189). Assertiveness, in time, should be as normal a part of our behaviour as indicating that you are pleased to see someone. It should be as easy to adopt if you choose.

If you adapt the techniques to suit yourself and your communication, you then have a greater range of skills that you can use to deal with difficult people. Any behaviour, which leads to the outcome that you want, can be 'right' and should be used. However, I have set out some of the behaviours that others use with me that triggers me to use assertion skills.

# ANGRY AND OTHER EMOTIONALLY UPSET PEOPLE

When you encounter someone who is emotionally upset, it is usually the best plan to find out the reasons as soon as you can and at the same time try to reduce the active emotion. I say usually, because you may occasionally be confronted with someone who is totally aggressive and threatens you with verbal abuse or physical violence. This is dealt with later.

In order to achieve these two immediate targets, you can use a combination of the techniques suggested in Chapters 4 and 5. If the person is upset and has not given you permission to talk about it, then a Conversation Opener (see pages 51–2) is needed to get their permission to establish limits. This can be used at any stage in the process if, in the course of your discussion, a possibly private or personal matter is uncovered. This may well happen, because the next and most important technique is to use Active (Reflective) Listening (see page 70). If the other person accosts you, you may still need their permission to continue in order to respect their limits.

Active listening is the skill that is most useful if you wish to reduce the emotional level in another person so that you can communicate with them rationally and logically. As stated, (page 72) it is the technique used by professionals:

- When they are trying to get the other person to identify the real problems without emotional bias or misunderstanding.
- To discover and keep on the other's wavelength by establishing common ground using empathy: understanding what somebody says they feel, without approval or condemnation.
- Thereby they keep the problem with the other person until they feel that they have fully grasped it.
- There is a joke, that at a certain therapy centre, when people come in and say, 'Good morning', all the therapists answer, 'So you feel it's a nice day?'

It is possible to get the impression that all you do when you are using Active Listening is to paraphrase the other person reflexively in your own words, so here are some guidelines:

- It is normally best not to interrupt the other person when they are in full flow. It is preferable to wait until they stop or pause, and then summarise what you think you have heard them say. This conveys understanding, or a statement that can be corrected. Also it enables the other person to hear what they have said and since you are trying to understand them, a chance to give you the real story; free from emotional bias.
- If you are learning, some people find themselves thinking so much about how and what they are going to reflect that they are not really listening (see Subconscious Competence, Chapter 14). The way to overcome this is not to worry

about the technique, but listen to what the other person is saying and, when they pause, summarise what you think they have said, including their feelings. This is essential because you use the technique to defuse their emotions.

There is nothing so good as being able to reflect what an emotional person has said until they say, 'That's it exactly', to settle or calm a person down. Frustration comes from not being heard or understood. Think about how you would react if somebody understood what you felt and were saying, to the point where you could say, 'You seem to understand me.' It usually makes people go on to reveal more, as they will to somebody on their wavelength. It is certainly what we need, when we have finished a hard, over-stressed day. Have you got someone who listens to your woes, without being judgemental or 'bettering' them?

There is also an advantage in that the other person, on having his or her words reflected as a statement of what they seem to have said, will modify their original statement, which may have been exaggerated to get your attention. Because you are listening to what they say, they can be more reasonable and factual. This is the powerful tool to defuse emotion. Try it and find out.

If you were to respond with only reflective statements, when someone communicated to you emotionally, it would be a rather artificial conversation. The technique involves using Acknowledgement Responses (see pages 64/65) to encourage the other person. And occasional Open and Specific Questions (see pages 53/54) to clarify your understanding before you can reflect back.

The majority of people I meet on my courses tell me that they can reflectively listen to each other. When I sit in, to listen and observe them in exercises, only about 5 per cent can really do it. The chief problem is that they are so very used to normal responses and possible remedies, that they interfere with what the other person is saying (see interference in empathetic conversation page 66).

The key is to concentrate 100 per cent on what the other person is saying and how they feel about it. This means trying to ignore any of your own thoughts that might pop into your head, except those which lead to the very occasional specific or open question to clarify some detail or feeling. At the end, to reflect a very short summary, include the strongest expressed feelings.

The objective is to be able to sum up and reflect back to the other person the real problem so that they say, 'Yes, that's it, exactly.' Up to this point you have been keeping the problem with them and it is time to consider your next step. Some options that you can consider are:

- To ask the other person what they would like to happen. Too often, people hear another's problems and try to suggest their own solutions. Ask yourself, if you have been stressed or upset about something, whether you got a response starting like 'What you should do is . . .'? It is generally much better to ask the other person what they want to happen, then if advice is sought later, it can be relevant and on the other person's wavelength. Managers have traditionally perceived their role as problem-solvers and people with answers. An advanced approach is to determine the other's wishes first.

- Sometimes, because of the situation, you are aware of the other's wishes (beware of assumption) and are sure that if you asked them their wishes, you know that it would fuel their expectations, which you realise you cannot fulfil. In this case, you can still ask them what they want: first, however, you state your limits and try to get their acceptance of them. The question is, what do they wish within your limits? This can be the first step towards getting a workable compromise (see page 34).

- It can be that the other person was stressed, and reflecting their problem back to them enables them to see the situation in a different light. In this case there is no other action to take, if they wish to think about it. Again, this can be determined by asking them.

- The other person may seem to want your solution or approach. In this case, you can determine this by asking them. It takes only a moment to say, 'Do you want to know what I think?'; 'Would you like my advice?'; 'Can I give you my thoughts or opinion?' This ensures that you are staying within permitted limits.

- Of course, it is much easier if the other person says, 'What do you think or want?' This gives you permission within the other's limit.

If you are confronted by somebody who is angry with you personally, you may get criticism. The other person may be annoyed with you personally, or it could be because you represent an organisation. Perhaps the other person has found fault with some goods or service supplied by that organisation. Whichever the case, you will need persistence (see 'Broken Record' page 78) and a means of not getting caught up in manipulative criticism and being diverted or 'hooked'. The last thing you need, if you want to use assertive behaviour, is to get caught up in an argument, to try to score points or hurt the other person. You have a range of techniques, depending on how you perceive the criticism.

If you think the criticism is intended to be hurtful

(beyond your limit), or you have a different point of view from that of the other person, then you can use 'Fogging' (see page 90). It is a title I don't like, because what you are trying to do is say that you honestly can appreciate the other person's point of view. There is a terrible cliché, 'I hear what you are saying', which is believed to have originated with lawyers. My technique is different, if used assertively, in that it is used honestly and says that not only do you hear them, but you are trying to understand them. It could be that the cliché is used genuinely, as a lawyer argued with me, but it tends to lose its credibility, as with saying 'with respect . . .' (see page 88). The essential thing is to try to find something in their point that you can partly agree with, however small, and return to the main point:

- 'I think you are * * * * * * * unreasonable/don't care!'
  - 'I am sure that we look that way to you, in this case . . .'
  - 'I can see why this is important/urgent to you, however I am obliged by law . . .'
  - 'Yes, from your point of view I might appear unreasonable/as though I don't care, in this instance . . .'
- 'What about the time you did . . .?'
  - 'Well, I may have been at fault there. However, this time . . .'
  - 'We have made mistakes in the past, in this case . . .'

and so on.

If it is possible, it is even better to be able to admit something specific. It is unusual behaviour in these days of 'double talk', when people, especially politicians, never admit that they have made mistakes. It gives you an advantage, if you can do it genuinely, without being over-apologetic. It removes the criticism that the other person was using to manipulate you. This technique is described as Negative Assertion (see page 91).

- 'What about the time you did . . .?'
  - 'Yes, I did make a mistake then. This time . . .'
  - 'I was wrong then. In this case . . .'

Both these approaches to dealing with criticism are to help you cope with it quickly, so that you are not distracted from your main purpose. Another technique, called Negative Enquiry (see page 93), spends more time on the criticism, because as it is presented you don't want to admit that they have a right to the view or admit any part of it. This is useful when criticism is generalised or judgemental, unsupported by facts. The technique is to ask for the evidence in a calm, interested way. You may learn that the criticism has some foundation and then reassess your responses:

- 'I think you are * * * * * * * unreasonable/don't care!'
  - 'Oh, perhaps you could tell me why you think this?'
  - 'Please tell why you say that.'

If there is no foundation for the criticism, then you are likely to be met by only more bluster, repetition or silence, at which point you can reflect the fact back and revert to your original theme.

Sometimes, if the criticism is plainly implausible, it is effective to reflect it back to the critic as a way of dealing with it originally.

- 'You've always hated me.'
  - 'So you feel that I have disliked you throughout our friendship?'

Also, occasionally, some people who are emotionally upset will be over-talkative. Finding someone on their wavelength, they keep on going over the same ground, because you are listening. This can happen to people who meet customers on reception desks at work. There can be a limit on their time and, sometimes, a queue of other increasingly impatient people, waiting to be dealt with. In this case it is possible to use the reflecting technique in the same way as an interim summary at a meeting. You interrupt and check that you have got the message so far, inviting the other person to add anything extra or new. The use of this technique has to be balanced with the skill of reducing the emotional level.

- 'Sorry to interrupt, but I would like to check that I have got all the details of what you've been saying.' – (Reflect) – 'Have I missed anything?'

## MANIPULATIVE PEOPLE

All of the skills that can be used to stop you being manipulated by emotionally upset people are equally relevant when dealing with manipulative people. There are a few tips to add to the section on 'Saying No' (page 131), something that non-assertive people find very difficult to do with manipulative people. How do we say no, reasonably and assertively?

The first step in deciding to agree to, or refuse, a request is to check a few factors:

- How strongly do you feel like saying no; are you hesitant?
- What is the specific issue; what are your rights; what is your preferred outcome and one you would accept?

- What is your programming; what are the real
  consequences of refusing; what are the consequences of not
  making your limits known?

If you would like more time to think about these factors,
then that is the next step. The same applies to asking for
more information about what is being asked of you.
Manipulators often try to rush non-assertive people into
overhasty decisions, leaving them to resent it afterwards.
Often a few moments of uninterrupted thought will suffice
for you to clarify these matters. Also, it can help to think
about what you are going to do and how you are going to
do it. For many people hearing and seeing themselves doing
things successfully in their minds before the event is
enormously helpful (see book list *Introducing NLP*). The
sorts of thing that you can think about at this stage are:

- Composing a short reason for refusing the request, which
  you feel happy with, such as: 'No, I can't stay late this
  evening, because I have made other plans, which I am not
  prepared to change at this notice.' The message must be
  one that you are happy with, in your own words, because
  if you are dealing with manipulation, you will have to
  persist with it. Also you will have to resist it being
  questioned, such as: 'Anyway, what are you doing that is
  so important?' You may well reply that is your private
  business and return to your message. You do not want to
  get into a debate about your choice of priorities. The
  reason has to be genuine (important to you, to want it as
  an outcome) and not just what one American President
  said: 'Watch my lips, NO!'
- The message should not be aggressive, because you are
  refusing the request not the person. If someone is trying to

manipulate you by using the previous relationship and favours that they have done for you, it is a reasonable tactic to state how much you appreciate this and state that it is not them personally, before repeating your message.

- It can also be useful to compose yourself, by thinking about your non-verbal communication, such as appearing calm, collected and sounding interested and reasonable. It is also helpful, if you are anxious about the prospect, to exhale deeply. This stops the build up of carbon dioxide in the bloodstream, which is one of the physiological causes of anxiety.

When you have stated your reason is the time that you will need all your skills of dealing with criticisms, either direct or implied; seeing their point of view; admitting the possibility of specific points; asking for detail; or reflecting. The important thing is not to be distracted from the proposal by side issues. Whereas, a short expression of understanding of the other person's position,

- 'I understand that this is important/urgent to you, however . . .'

is reasonable to keep some wavelength. Like apologising too much, it can be overdone and lead the other person (manipulative) to sense a weakness that they can exploit. Of course, being reasonable, you are prepared for a 'workable compromise'. This is the value of thinking about your preferred option and what you would settle for (see book list *Getting to Yes*).

- 'I am prepared to come in early tomorrow, if that will help.'

This must be reasonable and accepted by you.

## PEOPLE WHO ARE VIOLENT OR ABUSIVE

More people are now encountering verbal abuse or physical violence. It is easy to say avoid it, but for some this is easier said than done.

With verbal abuse, you have to make a judgement, very quickly, after a first attempt at reflecting, such as; 'You are very angry, because . . .' If you get a response like, 'Too right, I'll tell you about it', then you are on the right track. If you get more abuse, this means the other person does not respect your limits or your efforts. You have to be very aware of the reactions of the other person, rather than thinking about how you can pursue your purpose in communicating with them. You need to think of how, or if, you have any chance of reducing their emotional state.

If you decide that there is no point in continuing the communication then it is best to point this out. A statement, containing an ultimatum ('Consequences' page 153) can be used:

- 'If you continue to swear at me without listening to what I have to say, I see no point in continuing this conversation.'
- 'If we can't discuss this matter seriously, I can't see any reason to continue. I will have to leave. I would rather stay and talk reasonably.'

If the situation is one that frequently occurs, then it is as well to have thought of something that suits you and is effective beforehand. Some organisations have standard responses, but unless you are an actor and can make it sound natural, it is better to adapt it to yourself.

With violence, unless you are supremely confident of your ability to restrain the other person, it is better to use avoidance behaviour. Even if you feel that physically you can cope, to be assertive successfully afterwards is very difficult.

• I can only number one occasion in my life, where afterwards there was better understanding and respect for each other's limits.

If you are in a position where you are likely to encounter violence, it is better to think out your responses and actions in advance. How can you ensure your safety? What action will you then take?

• Somebody very close to me rang up to say that she had been hit in a fit of jealousy. After listening to her concerns, the facts and her feelings, I asked her what she wanted to do. She asked me what I thought, because she had liked the previous relationship and thought she ought to forgive and forget. I said that, if it were me, I would be afraid that this submissive, rewarding behaviour would be likely to be repeated. Did she want that, or how could she ensure it didn't happen?

Once is more than too much. Violence against a person shows a lack of respect that no assertive technique can overcome, until it has been quelled, or subsided, and the other person is willing to listen to you reasonably. Often, flight is the best immediate response, never mind conditioning and pride. And then thinking very seriously about how you can avoid such incidents; can you take action to ensure it?

- I am disturbed, because I have recently seen two young children, of rational age and behaviour, hit their mothers quite aggressively, because their wishes were thwarted. And they then continued, without remonstration (limits), as though nothing had occurred.

It is worth thinking about how you would try to cope with violence, if you are in a position to meet many different people and what action you would take afterwards. Best of all is to anticipate possible occasions and avoid them, or take such actions as will secure your safety.

## SILENT PEOPLE

I have included silent people in the list of difficult people, because some people find them problematic. It all depends on why they are silent. The shy people can be encouraged with Conversation Skills (see Chapter 4) and being prepared to wait out their silences, so that they have time to think.

It is the insolent or aggressive silence that worries some. One of the effective responses to this is to treat it as a reply. We communicate mainly with our body language, whether we speak or not (see page 103). It is perfectly reasonable to say:

- 'I take it from your lack of response that . . .'
- 'Because you walked away, I will assume . . .'

This is not reflecting in that the thoughts come from you, but in the absence of communication it is an attempt to start constructive dialogue, as long as the observations are not aggressive and go over the other person's permitted limits. That would show a lack of respect and, if you think of it, all the people that you respect, respect you.

# BOOKS THAT I HAVE FOUND USEFUL

John Adair, *Effective Leadership* (Pan Books).
A great guide to what you have to do in leadership. I hope my book gives some indication as to how to do it.

Ken and Kate Back, *Assertiveness at Work: A practical guide to handling awkward situations* (McGraw Hill).
A very detailed analysis of assertiveness. Particularly good on 'inner dialogues'.

Tony Buzan, *Make the Most of Your Mind* (Pan Books).
A book I cannot praise enough. It all works.

Eric Berne, *Games People Play* (Penguin Books).
An excellent American book, explaining Transactional Analysis. This is followed by a detailed account of the many manipulative ploys and tactics that people use, in different relationships, to get the responses that they want from others.

Manuel J. Smith, *When I Say No I Feel Guilty* (Bantam Books).
An original, good and detailed American analysis of our rights and how to use assertive skills to cope with every-day situations. I do have reservations about the second

'assertive right'; that you have the right to offer no reasons or excuses to justify your behaviour, because, on many occasions, this can be aggressive and not reasonable behaviour in our culture.

**Robert Sharpe, *Assert Yourself* (Kogan Page).**
A very therapeutic-styled book, which deals with how to improve your relationships and image with others. Again, I am not happy with the list of rights for our culture: '3 The right to make decisions or statements without having to justify them; and 10 The right to do all of these things without giving any reason at all for your actions'. These are too sweeping as statements and include aggressive behaviour, as well as assertion. They can not be reasonable, although the author goes on to say if 'We break social or behavioral rules,' under exploitative circumstances, 'we must be responsible for our actions.' In so much as aggression can be the best choice of behaviour, I agree, but the 'right' as stated is inclusive.

**Ursula Markham, *How To Deal with Difficult People* (Thorsons).**
A good book, which puts people into types and tells you how to handle them with assertive techniques.

**Roger Fisher, William Ury and Bruce Patton, *Getting To Yes* (Century).**
The skills of negotiation. Invaluable.

**William Ury, *Getting Past No* (Century).**
Negotiating with difficult people.

Joseph O'Connor and John Seymour, *Introducing NLP (Neuro-Linguistic Programming)* (Aquarian Press).
A good, comprehensive and understandable book on psychological skills, understanding and influencing people and developing your talents.

Charles Handy, *Gods of Management* (Souvenir Press).
Analyses the different cultures of organisations in an original way.

Charles Handy, *The Age of Unreason* (Arrow).
Analyses the way organisations and working practices are changing and the effects of this on employees.

Thomas Harris, *I'm OK, You're OK* (Arrow).
A great insight into how we and others can use Transactional Analysis to help, or hinder, our success in our lives.

# INDEX